The Book On Relationships

How We Connect, Why We Hurt, and What Love Can Become

The Book On Series

C.S. Morgan

Published by The Book On Publishing, 2025.
First edition. May 20, 2025.

I0459024

Website: https://thebookon.ca

Substack: https://thebookonpublishing.substack.com/

RELATIONSHIPS: HOW WE CONNECT, WHY WE HURT, AND WHAT LOVE CAN BECOME

First edition. May 20, 2025.

Copyright © 2025 The Book On Publishing

ISBN: 978-1-997795-81-0

Written by C.S. Morgan.

The Book On Series

The Book On Life Unscripted

The Book On Risk Management in Payments

The Book On AI for Everyday People

The Book On Relationships

The Book On Master The Algorithm

The Book On Saying No

The Book On Community Led Strategy

The Book On The Myth of Multitasking

The Book On The Burnout Blueprint

The Book On The Digital Reboot

The Book On The Shape of What's Coming

The Book On Strategic Obsession

The Book On High-Stakes Thinking

The Book On Artificial Leverage

The Book On Clarity

The Book On Uncertainty

The Book On Operational Excellence

The Book On Escape

Dear Reader,

If you've made it to this page, thank you. Truly. Writing about love—something so personal, layered, and tender—is one thing. But sharing it with strangers and trusting it will reach the right hands? That takes trust. And I don't take it lightly.

Maybe you picked up this book during a breakup. Or in the middle of a relationship, you're still trying to understand. Perhaps you're single and figuring things out, or years into a love that still asks you to grow. Wherever you are, I hope you felt seen—not in a tidy, polished way, but in a human one.

These pages weren't written to teach you how to love like someone else. They were written to help you love like *you*. With your fears, quirks, longings, and history. With everything you've carried, and everything you're still trying to set down.

I hope you leave this book not with answers, but with better questions. Not with rules, but with more curiosity. And above all, knowing love isn't reserved for those who get it "right." It belongs to all of us who are willing to try.

Thank you for letting me walk a little of the way with you.

With care,

C.S. Morgan

Table of Contents

CHAPTER 1: THE RELATIONSHIP MIRROR 11

    INTRODUCTION.. 11

    REFLECTIONS WE DON'T RECOGNIZE 11

    CHILDHOOD BLUEPRINTS 12

    SEEING WITHOUT DISTORTION 14

    REFLECTION 16

CHAPTER 2: THE NEED TO BELONG......................................18

    INTRODUCTION.. 18

    THE ACHE WE CARRY 18

    THE SCIENCE OF CONNECTION 19

    FINDING BELONGING WITHOUT DISAPPEARING 21

    REFLECTION 23

CHAPTER 3: LOVE ISN'T WHAT WE THOUGHT 25

    INTRODUCTION.. 25

    THE FAIRYTALE WE INHERITED... 25

    ROMANCE VERSUS REALITY.. 26

    LOVE ISN'T A FEELING, IT'S A PRACTICE 28

    REFLECTION 30

CHAPTER 4: ATTRACTION, CHEMISTRY, AND TIMING.......................32

    INTRODUCTION.. 32

    THE PUZZLE OF PREFERENCE 32

    CHEMISTRY IS REAL, BUT IT'S NOT EVERYTHING 34

    TIMING ISN'T JUST CIRCUMSTANCE, IT'S CHARACTER 35

    REFLECTION 38

CHAPTER 5: ATTACHMENT – THE INVISIBLE SCRIPT..........................39

    INTRODUCTION.. 39

    THE BLUEPRINT WE DIDN'T KNOW WE HAD............................... 40

    WHY WE REPEAT WHAT HURTS US 41

    BECOMING SECURE, EVEN IF YOU DIDN'T START THAT WAY 42

    REFLECTION 44

CHAPTER 6: COMMUNICATION OR THE LACK THEREOF 46

    INTRODUCTION.. 46

    SPEAKING WITHOUT SAYING MUCH 46

Listening Without Really Hearing 48

When Silence Becomes a Language 49

Reflection 52

CHAPTER 7: THE POWER OF VULNERABILITY 54

Introduction... 54

The Armor We Learn to Wear 54

The Risk of Being Seen.. 55

Staying Open Without Losing Yourself... 57

Reflection 59

CHAPTER 8: BOUNDARIES – THE BRIDGE AND THE WALL 61

Introduction... 61

What's Yours and What's Theirs 61

Saying No Without Losing Love 62

Respecting Other People's Boundaries... 64

Reflection 66

CHAPTER 9: THE STORIES WE CARRY 68

Introduction... 68

Inheriting What Was Never Ours 68

The Role We Played, and Still Play.. 69

Rewriting the Narrative 70

Reflection 73

CHAPTER 10: SEX, AFFECTION, AND DESIRE 75

Introduction... 75

More Than Just a Physical Act... 75

When Desire Changes 76

The Affection We Don't Talk About... 78

Reflection 80

CHAPTER 11: CONFLICT AS A DOORWAY 82

Introduction... 82

What We're Fighting About 79

The Way We Fight Matters More Than Why 84

The Art of Repair... 85

Reflection 87

CHAPTER 12: GROWING TOGETHER (OR APART) 89

Introduction... 89

Change Is Not a Betrayal... 89

WHEN ONE GROWS FASTER THAN THE OTHER 90

STAYING, LEAVING, OR REIMAGINING 92

REFLECTION 93

CHAPTER 13: THE ROLE OF TRUST 95

INTRODUCTION.. 95

THE SLOW BUILD 95

WHEN TRUST BREAKS.. 96

REBUILDING, IF YOU CHOOSE TO 97

REFLECTION 100

CHAPTER 14: FRIENDSHIP AS FOUNDATION 102

INTRODUCTION.. 102

THE OVERLOOKED INGREDIENT 102

WHEN FRIENDSHIP FADES 103

HOW TO BE LOVERS AND FRIENDS.. 104

REFLECTION 107

CHAPTER 15: LOVE IN THE DIGITAL AGE 109

INTRODUCTION.. 109

SWIPE CULTURE AND THE ILLUSION OF INFINITE CHOICE 109

CONNECTION VS. CONTACT.. 111

GHOSTING, BREADCRUMBING, AND THE FEAR OF BEING TOO MUCH 112

PRESENCE IN A WORLD OF DISTRACTION 114

REFLECTION 116

CHAPTER 16: LOVE ACROSS DIFFERENCES 118

INTRODUCTION.. 118

DIFFERENCE ISN'T THE PROBLEM, AVOIDANCE IS.................................... 118

POWER, PRIVILEGE, AND THE SPACE BETWEEN 119

WHEN VALUES CLASH AND CONVERSATIONS GET HARD............................ 121

BUILDING A SHARED LANGUAGE 122

REFLECTION 124

CHAPTER 17: FAMILY, CHILDREN, AND THE SHIFTING CENTER 126

INTRODUCTION.. 126

WHEN CHILDREN CHANGE EVERYTHING 126

THE PULL OF EXTENDED FAMILY 128

FINDING EACH OTHER AGAIN AFTER EVERYTHING 129

REFLECTION 132

CHAPTER 18: BREAKUPS AND ENDINGS 134

INTRODUCTION 134

THE DECISION TO LEAVE 134

GRIEVING WHAT MIGHT HAVE BEEN 135

ENDING WITHOUT DESTROYING 137

REFLECTION 139

CHAPTER 19: THE WORK OF LONG, TERM LOVE **141**

INTRODUCTION 141

LOVING THE SAME PERSON OVER AND OVER AGAIN 141

THE MYTH OF EFFORTLESS LOVE 142

RITUAL, RENEWAL, AND THE SMALL THINGS THAT MATTER 144

REFLECTION 147

CHAPTER 20: THE RELATIONSHIP WITH YOURSELF **148**

INTRODUCTION 148

THE MIRROR YOU CAN'T ESCAPE 148

SOLITUDE ISN'T EMPTINESS 149

COMING HOME TO YOURSELF 150

REFLECTION 152

CHAPTER 21: THE REBUILD **154**

INTRODUCTION 154

THE MOMENT YOU STOP PRETENDING 154

WHAT YOU GAVE UP WITHOUT REALIZING 155

THE PRACTICE OF RETURNING 157

CHOOSING AGAIN 158

REFLECTION 159

CONCLUSION **161**

LOVE IS THE WORK AND THE REWARD 161

Dedication

For anyone who's ever felt like too much, or not enough,

for the ones who stayed, the ones who left,

and the ones still learning how to come home to themselves.

This book is for you.

Because love, in all its forms, begins there.

-    C. S. Morgan

-

In the quiet ache of embrace, the need to belong finds its most honest expression—raw, unspoken, and deeply human. We are shaped by the arms that hold us and fractured by their absence.

Chapter 1: The Relationship Mirror

How our connections reflect, shape, and challenge who we are.

Introduction

We often think of relationships as separate from us, external events we step into, hoping for the best. But the truth is, every connection is a reflection. Not just of who we are, but of who we've been taught to be, what we fear, what we long for, and what we believe we're worth. Relationships are rarely just about the other person. They are places where we meet ourselves.

This chapter explores the role relationships play in shaping our identity, starting with the earliest ones we form, and tracing how those patterns echo through our adult lives. We'll examine how other people become our mirrors, and what it takes to see our reflection clearly without mistaking it for the whole truth.

Reflections We Don't Recognize

Imagine standing in front of someone you love and realizing that your reaction to them — anger, anxiety, jealousy, or deep affection — is less about them and more about what they activate inside you. It's unsettling. We spend so much time assuming that the people around us cause our feelings. But the truth is more complicated, and also more empowering.

That frustration you felt when your partner didn't respond the way you wanted might not be about their response at all. It might be about your history with rejection. Your reaction to a friend pulling away might not be about their absence but about a childhood experience of being left behind. In this way, people become mirrors, reflecting wounds we thought we buried, stories we tell ourselves, and roles we unconsciously replay.

The most vivid reflections come from the relationships that feel intense. The ones that stir something. It's no coincidence. The people who draw out the most emotion often mirror something unresolved in us. That's why it's not always the kindest or compatible people who leave a mark; it's the ones who mirror a part of us we haven't yet come to terms with.

But this doesn't mean relationships are doomed to repeat old stories. If we learn to look closely at what we're feeling, not just at what the other person is doing, we gain insight. We start to see how the stories we carry distort the mirrors we look into. And with enough awareness, we can change what we reflect.

Childhood Blueprints

Every relationship we have is shaped by the first ones we knew. Before we even had language, we were absorbing patterns, watching how our caregivers responded to our cries, how safe it felt to express need, how available or distant love seemed. These early dynamics don't just fade with time. They become scripts.

Some of us grew up in homes where love meant caretaking. We learned that we had to earn affection by being helpful, cheerful, or invisible. Others knew that love was conditional, given and taken away based on performance or mood. Still others experienced love as chaotic or absent, unpredictable or even frightening. These early experiences didn't just teach us about love. They taught us about ourselves.

When we carry these blueprints into adulthood, we often don't realize we're acting them out. We may find ourselves drawn to people who feel familiar, even if that familiarity brings pain. We may believe that relationships are inherently unstable, or that we must sacrifice our needs to stay connected. And because these patterns are unconscious, we often repeat them without recognizing the choice.

But here's the liberating truth: the blueprint isn't fixed. Relationships that reflect our patterns can also help us rewrite them. When we encounter someone who responds differently, who stays calm when we expect conflict, who offers closeness instead of withdrawal, it's disorienting. And it's healing. We realize the mirror can show us not just where we've been, but where we might go.

Seeing Without Distortion

Not every mirror tells the truth. Just like in a funhouse, relationships can distort reality. Sometimes we project our fears onto others, seeing betrayal in neutrality or indifference in distraction. Other times, we idealize someone, believing they are everything we've ever wanted, only to be disappointed when their humanity shows through.

The distortion isn't always in the other person. Often, it's in the lens we're using. If we view every interaction through the fog of past pain, we're bound to misread the present. If we're waiting for abandonment, we'll interpret even small acts of independence as signs of rejection. And if we carry a belief that we're unworthy of love, we'll mistrust anyone who offers it freely.

The task, then, is to clean the mirror. To distinguish between what is happening and what our history makes us fear is happening. That requires slowing down. Paying attention not just to what others are doing, but to what we're telling ourselves about it. It means asking: "Is this true now, or is this a memory disguised as the present?"

As we learn to see more clearly, relationships become less about reactivity and more about reflection. We can still feel hurt or triggered, but we respond with curiosity instead of blame. We start choosing partners, friends, and patterns more consciously. The mirror, once a source of confusion, becomes a tool for growth.

Case Study: *Dani and the Echo*

Dani had a type. They didn't know it at first, not in the way people say they're drawn to a particular look or profession, but they noticed a pattern when the same ache kept returning at the end of every relationship.

Each partner was different on paper. One was a writer. One was an introverted math teacher. Another was a brilliant extrovert who filled every room with charm. But the common thread wasn't in who these people were. It was in how Dani felt around them, as if they were constantly reaching out. Always trying to prove they were enough.

When Dani's third serious relationship in four years ended with the exact words, "You're just a lot", something cracked. Not in a catastrophic way, but in the slow, sobering realization that maybe the relationships weren't the problem. Perhaps the echo was coming from inside.

They started therapy. Not to figure out what was wrong with their exes, but to understand why they kept abandoning themselves in the name of staying close. What they uncovered wasn't dramatic. It was ordinary, which made it harder to see. Dani grew up with a single parent who was loving but distracted. Emotionally unavailable. Not cruel, just consumed by survival. Dani learned to be "low maintenance," managing their feelings quietly and only needing affection when it was convenient.

In adulthood, that same pattern played out. Dani gravitated toward people who didn't have much to give emotionally and then worked overtime trying to earn scraps of intimacy. It wasn't love they were chasing. It was familiarity.

The turning point didn't come from a new partner. It came from Dani sitting in a coffee shop, alone, after another breakup, asking not, "Why didn't they love me better?" but, "Why do I keep loving like this hurts less than being alone?"

That question became a mirror.

Years later, Dani did fall in love again. But this time, they noticed the difference. The love didn't feel like striving. It felt like breathing. And when that familiar urge to earn affection crept in, Dani didn't ignore it. They held it gently and said, "I see you. But I don't need to perform anymore."

Reflection

What mirror did you notice in your last relationship?

Sometimes, the loneliest place is the one where we finally meet ourselves.

Chapter 2: The Need to Belong

Why connection matters more than we admit, and what happens when we're without it.

Introduction

We are wired to connect. Before we learned to speak, we reached for our caregivers. Before we learned to reason, we cried out for closeness. This need, to be seen, held, and understood, is not a weakness. It's not something to "get over" in the name of independence. It's a fundamental part of what it means to be human.

In this chapter, we'll explore what belonging means, why its absence feels so sharp, and how our relationships rise and fall on our ability to connect meaningfully. Loneliness isn't just an emotional ache. It's a signal. And when we learn to respond to that signal with curiosity and compassion, we stop treating connection like a luxury and start recognizing it as a need worth honoring.

The Ache We Carry

There's a specific kind of pain that doesn't show up on X-rays. You can't measure it in broken bones or bruised skin, but you feel it deep in the chest, like a hollowness. That pain is loneliness. And for all our talk about productivity, independence, and self-sufficiency, loneliness remains one of the most common and least spoken of human experiences.

You can be surrounded by people and still feel utterly alone. You can be married, admired, even celebrated, and still ache for a kind of closeness that feels just out of reach. This is because loneliness isn't about proximity. It's about resonance. We feel lonely when we can't find someone who understands us, not just intellectually, but emotionally, when we feel like we're speaking into a void, unheard and unseen.

The irony is that so many of us are feeling this, silently, at the same time. We scroll through curated lives on social media, assuming everyone else is connected. We mistake visibility for intimacy, attention for affection. And so we retreat further, ashamed of our need, fearing it makes us weak or broken.

But needing connection doesn't make us fragile. It makes us human. And when we learn to name that need without shame, we stop reaching unquestioningly and start reaching wisely. We stop filling the void with performance, distraction, or overcommitment, and begin to ask for what nourishes us.

The Science of Connection

For a long time, we've treated emotional needs as optional, like accessories to the more "serious" business of work, survival, or achievement. But the body tells a different story. Studies have shown that loneliness activates the same neural pathways as physical pain. Our nervous systems register disconnection not as an inconvenience, but as a threat.

From an evolutionary perspective, this makes sense. Humans survived not because we were the fastest or strongest species, but because we were cooperative. Belonging wasn't a preference; it was survival. To be cast out from the group meant danger. To be touched, nurtured, and protected meant life.

This wiring hasn't gone away. Today, when we feel isolated or rejected, our cortisol levels spike. Our sleep suffers. Our immune systems weaken. The effects of prolonged loneliness have been compared to smoking a pack of cigarettes a day in terms of health impact. But it goes beyond biology.

Emotionally, disconnection chips away at our sense of self. If no one sees us, do we still matter? If our inner world is invisible to others, how do we trust that it's real? Connection isn't just about comfort; it's about coherence. When someone mirrors our feelings, when they nod and say "me too," we don't just feel supported, we feel sane.

That's why healthy relationships are healing. Not because they "fix" us, but because they remind us we're not alone in the way we suffer, dream, or hope.

Finding Belonging Without Disappearing

The paradox of belonging is that it's both a surrender and a declaration. On one hand, we open ourselves up to being shaped by others. We soften, compromise, and allow space for someone else in our story. On the other hand, true belonging requires that we not lose ourselves in the process. That we don't become so shapeshifted by others that we forget who we were before they arrived.

This is the tightrope many of us struggle to walk. In our hunger for connection, we sometimes trade authenticity for approval. We say what we think the other person wants to hear. We dim parts of ourselves to avoid conflict. We perform roles, charming, agreeable, selfless, not because they reflect who we are, but because they seem more palatable. But a connection built on performance is always brittle.

Belonging, real belonging, doesn't require us to be perfect. It asks us to be present. It doesn't demand we be easy to love, only that we show up honestly, even if our truth is messy or complicated. That kind of vulnerability can be terrifying, especially if past attempts at honesty were met with rejection. But the only way to truly feel loved is to let yourself be truly seen.

When we find people who let us be fully ourselves, flawed, growing, sometimes confused, we see not just safety, but strength. Belonging becomes not a mask we wear, but a mirror of our most genuine self.

Case Study: Cam and the Empty Room

People always surrounded Cam. In university, they were the friend everyone called for a ride home, the group project leader, and the host of every birthday dinner. Their phone was never silent, and their calendar was never empty. But deep down, they felt something they couldn't name, an invisible emptiness that followed them from room to room.

It wasn't that they were unloved. People liked Cam. Trusted Cam. But no one *knew* Cam. They played the role they thought was safest: reliable, funny, never too emotional. Cam had become the person who made sure everyone else felt like they belonged, without ever asking if they did.

The moment of reckoning came after a personal loss. Cam's grandmother passed away, the only person in their life who had truly seen them without needing anything in return. Cam waited for someone to ask how they were doing. To show up. But the calls never came. Not because people didn't care, but because no one knew Cam was hurting. They hadn't let them.

That night, Cam sat alone in their apartment and finally admitted, "I feel invisible in rooms full of people I love."

It wasn't dramatic. It was honest.

That realization was the beginning of change. Slowly, Cam began letting small pieces of themselves surface. They told a friend they were struggling. They admitted they didn't want to host this time. They practiced saying, "I need support" without apology.

The surprising part? No one turned away. Some were even relieved. "I always thought you had it all figured out," one friend said. "But I'm glad you're letting me in."

Cam says belonging now feels less like performance and more like presence—less about being invited and more about being real.

They still have their big friend group. But now, they also have three people they can cry in front of. Laugh unfiltered with. Sit in silence beside. That, Cam says, is what it means to belong.

Reflection

Recall a moment you felt truly seen. What made it possible?

Real love begins where the fantasy ends, where we stop performing and start being.

Chapter 3: Love Isn't What We Thought

Unlearning the myths, fantasies, and cultural scripts that quietly shape our expectations of love.

Introduction

We grow up surrounded by stories about love. Fairy tales, romantic comedies, song lyrics, and social media each offer a version of what love is supposed to look like. We're taught to chase grand gestures, sudden certainty, and perfect matches. And we internalize these ideas without realizing it.

But real love rarely fits the mold. It's not always euphoric. It doesn't arrive on schedule or look the way we imagined. This chapter peels back the layers of fantasy to explore what love is, not the idealized version we're sold, but the messy, magnificent, grounding kind that grows when we let go of the script and start paying attention to what's real.

The Fairytale We Inherited

Somewhere along the way, many of us were handed a script. It went something like this: Love is a lightning bolt. You'll know it instantly. When it's right, it's easy. Your other half will arrive, complete you, and everything will finally make sense. And if it doesn't feel like that, it's not real.

It's a beautiful idea, tidy, comforting, cinematic. But it's also dangerously misleading.

Because in reality, most love doesn't strike like lightning. It unfolds slowly. It stumbles. It asks for patience. People aren't puzzle pieces waiting to be slotted into each other's lives. We are entire worlds, with complicated histories, shifting moods, and imperfect communication. We don't complete each other; we challenge, inspire, frustrate, and grow alongside one another.

When we cling too tightly to the fairytale, we start to mistrust the real thing. We question a relationship because it doesn't feel like fireworks every day. We doubt a partner because they don't finish our sentences or read our minds. And when conflict arises, as it always does, we panic. "This must not be the one," we tell ourselves. "Love isn't supposed to be this hard."

But the problem isn't that love is hard. It's what we expected it not to be. Love asks something of us that fairytales never do: to stay when it's uncomfortable. To be curious when we're confused. To love someone not for how they fulfill our fantasies, but for how they stand beside us in the truth of everyday life.

Romance Versus Reality

There's a moment in almost every new relationship when the shine begins to wear off. It's not that the person changes, it's that your vision clears. You start to notice the quirks that once seemed endearing now sometimes irritate you. You have your first fundamental disagreement. The novelty fades, and what's left is something more complex and more revealing.

This transition is often misunderstood. We're conditioned to believe that the spark should stay lit indefinitely, that excitement equals love, and that comfort signals complacency. So when the highs settle, we assume something's wrong. We long for the early rush and wonder if we've made a mistake.

But this is precisely where love begins, not the fantasy, but the reality. The moment when both people are no longer performing their best selves every day. When the masks drop, and we begin to see not just who the other person is, but who we are with them.

Real love lives here, in the space between effort and ease. It's not the constant high of infatuation, but the steady presence of someone who chooses you even after knowing your contradictions. It's not about being swept off your feet; it's about standing side by side, learning each other's rhythms, and building something that lasts beyond the rush.

The truth is, romance doesn't die; it matures. It becomes less about chasing novelty and more about deepening intimacy. A quiet hand on your back when you're anxious. A shared look across the table that says, "I'm still here." These moments don't make for blockbuster movies. But they're what real love is made of.

Love Isn't a Feeling, It's a Practice

Ask most people what love is, and you'll hear things like "butterflies," "chemistry," or "just knowing." Rarely do we describe love as a verb. But that's what it truly is: not just something you feel, but something you do.

Feelings come and go. Sleep, stress, hormones, and memory shape them. But actions, especially the small, consistent ones, build the foundation of lasting relationships. Love is listening even when you're tired. It's showing up even when you're annoyed. It's choosing care over convenience.

That doesn't mean love should feel like a chore. But when we reframe it as a daily practice, we liberate ourselves from the exhausting need to constantly "feel" in love. We stop panicking on the hard days. We understand that love isn't gone just because we're having a bad week; it's in how we navigate that week together.

This shift also gives us agency. Instead of waiting to be overwhelmed by passion, we become active participants in building connection. We ask better questions. We express needs clearly. We invest in rituals that sustain intimacy. Love becomes less about waiting and more about creating.

Perhaps the greatest myth of all is that love happens to us, like the weather. In truth, love is something we make, moment by moment, choice by choice. And in learning to love deliberately, we step into a version of love that's stronger, more flexible, and far more real than anything the fairytales prepared us for.

Case Study: Elena and the Fairytale Script

Elena believed in "The One." She grew up on a steady diet of romantic comedies and advice from older women that sounded like prophecy: "When you know, you know." "Love means never having to ask." "If it's meant to be, it'll just work."

So when she met Marco at twenty-seven, intelligent, charismatic, and spontaneous, it felt like fate. Their chemistry was instant. They moved in after three months and started planning a life. And at first, it felt like the movies promised: thrilling, magical, full of spontaneous laughter and late-night conversations.

But six months in, things started shifting. Marco wasn't cruel, but he was inconsistent. He pulled away when she needed reassurance. He dismissed her concerns as "too much." He avoided hard conversations, saying, "Why ruin the vibe?"

Still, Elena stayed. Because in her mind, this was supposed to be it. The story she had told herself for years said that real love was messy but worth it. Those butterflies meant destiny. That love meant *staying*, even when it hurt.

When she finally left, after a year and a half of shrinking, spinning, and second-guessing, Elena didn't feel triumphant. She felt like she had failed at a role she was supposed to master. She wasn't just grieving the relationship. She was grieving the *story*.

Therapy helped, but the bigger shift came on a solo weekend trip she booked to clear her head. Sitting on a beach with no one to perform for, Elena wrote a new question in her journal: *What if love isn't magic? What if it's a skill?*

That question became her compass. She began studying not love stories, but genuine relationships. She read about communication, boundaries, and repair. She looked at her past partners not as villains, but as mirrors for the parts of herself that had longed to be chosen by someone else.

Now, Elena says she doesn't want a soulmate. She wants a partner—someone to practice with. Someone to *build* love with, not discover it like buried treasure. She doesn't get butterflies anymore. But she gets calm. Safety. Growth.

And that, she says, feels better than any fairytale.

Reflection

Which romantic myth have you believed, and how has it served or limited you?

Attraction isn't random; it's a map of memory, chemistry, and the timing of who we are when we first feel seen.

Chapter 4: Attraction, Chemistry, and Timing

The surprising reasons we fall for certain people, and what that says about us.

Introduction

Attraction feels like magic, sudden, electric, impossible to explain. Chemistry can be instant or slow, burning, mysterious, or maddening. But beneath the surface, there's always a reason. We may not consciously understand why we're drawn to certain people, but our choices are rarely random.

This chapter dives into the hidden logic of attraction. How timing, familiarity, biology, and personal history intersect to create the gravitational pull we often mistake for fate. Love may be poetic, but it's also patterned, and when we begin to see the outlines of those patterns, we can learn to choose more wisely, love more clearly, and break free of the invisible strings pulling us toward the same kinds of people again and again.

The Puzzle of Preference

Have you ever found yourself irresistibly drawn to someone you couldn't explain? They didn't look like the kind of person you usually go for. Maybe you didn't even particularly like them at first. And yet, something hooked you. A glance. A laugh. A feeling in your chest that said, "Pay attention."

That's the strange power of attraction. It doesn't follow logic or checklist compatibility. It doesn't care about timing or even wisdom. It shows up like a whisper in the body, like a door swinging open without a sound.

But attraction is not random. It's memory. Our preferences, who we're drawn to and why, are shaped by a cocktail of familiarity, fantasy, and unconscious longing. Often, we're drawn to people who remind us of home. Not necessarily the safe, happy version of home, but the emotional blueprint we carry from childhood. If love was unpredictable growing up, we might find ourselves drawn to inconsistency, mistaking volatility for passion. If love feels distant, we may chase unavailable people, convinced that winning their affection will make us whole.

This is why chemistry can be confusing. It doesn't always signal health. Sometimes, it signals repetition. And while it's tempting to interpret strong attraction as proof of destiny, it's often more helpful to ask: What is familiar about this feeling? What part of me is being activated?

When we start asking those questions, we become more conscious participants in our own stories. Attraction doesn't lose its magic. It just becomes less of a mystery and more of a map.

Chemistry Is Real, but It's Not Everything

There's something undeniably powerful about chemistry. That invisible force that makes conversation effortless, touches electric, silence comfortable. It's thrilling to find someone whose presence makes you feel alive. But chemistry alone isn't a foundation. It's an invitation.

What we call "chemistry" is often a complex interplay of biology and emotion. Pheromones, voice pitch, facial symmetry, even how someone smells, all of it plays a role. So do deeper cues: how someone listens, the energy they carry, whether they mirror our expressions. Our nervous system picks up on these things instantly, even if we don't consciously understand them. That flutter in your chest isn't imaginary. It's your body reacting to a thousand signals at once.

But here's the trap: when we prioritize chemistry above all else, we risk ignoring compatibility. Just because someone makes your heart race doesn't mean they'll show up when it matters. Just because a conversation flows doesn't mean the values align. Chemistry is the spark, but relationships are built in the fire afterward, in the choices, the consistency, the daily effort to understand one another.

Many of us pursue chemistry because we believe it ensures a deeper connection. But over time, chemistry fades. Not entirely, but it softens. And what's left is the truth: the person behind the feeling. Who they are when they're tired. How they respond to conflict. Whether they're willing to grow with you.

That's where lasting love lives, not in the lightning strike, but in the slow, steady fire that follows. Chemistry may bring you together, but it's compatibility that keeps you there.

Timing Isn't Just Circumstance, It's Character

We like to think love is all about connection, that if two people genuinely care for one another, they'll make it work. But timing is more than logistics. It's readiness. Its capacity. It's the version of ourselves we bring into the relationship.

You can meet the right person at the wrong time. You can care deeply for someone and still not be able to love them well. You might be too angry. Too afraid. Too focused on healing from something else. Or maybe they are. Sometimes, the obstacle isn't a lack of love; it's that one or both people are still becoming the version of themselves they'd need to be to make love sustainable.

This is one of the most brutal truths to accept: that timing is not just about external life events, it's about emotional availability. About self-awareness. About the willingness to meet another person not with potential, but with presence.

In our more romantic moments, we like to believe love will wait. But in reality, it often moves on. Not out of cruelty, but necessity. Relationships require alignment, not just in desire, but in pace. If one person is sprinting and the other is standing still, they will not end up in the same place.

This doesn't mean that love lost to timing was meaningless. On the contrary, those relationships often teach us the most. They show us what we're capable of, what we long for, and what we need to become to love better next time.

Because in the end, love is as much about readiness as it is about chemistry. And when both arrive at the exact moment, when two people meet not just each other, but themselves, something remarkable can begin.

Case Study: Mateo, Harper, and the Lightning Strike

Mateo met Harper at a friend's rooftop party one humid August night. There was no easing in, only the jolt of instant recognition. Conversation flowed like they'd rehearsed it in another life. When Harper laughed, Mateo felt it in his knees. When Mateo touched Harper's wrist to make a point, electricity flickered up both their arms. Friends teased them, "Get a room!", and they didn't even blush. It felt inevitable.

Within a week, they were inseparable. Dates blurred into dawn drives; texts became novels. Neither had eaten nor appropriately slept in days, but neither cared. They called it love.

Yet beneath the blaze, real life waited. Mateo had just quit a draining consulting job to figure out what came next. He was raw, uncertain, secretly terrified of empty calendars. Harper, fresh out of a long relationship, had promised herself a year of solo travel and self-focus. But the chemistry convinced them both: *If it's this strong, we'll make it work.*

The cracks showed by month three. Harper's apartment lease was ending; she bought a one-way ticket to Lisbon, part dream, part escape. Mateo panicked: "Love doesn't pause." Harper countered: "If it's real, it survives space." They attempted to merge their plans, having loosely committed to reunite abroad, yet neither felt entirely solid in their decision.

Their last night together was both tender and strained. Harper cried in Mateo's arms; Mateo said he understood, though a knot sat in his throat. The next morning, they kissed at the airport gate, half promise, half goodbye.

Distance exposed what chemistry had eclipsed: Mateo wasn't ready to anchor anyone; Harper wasn't prepared to stay. Time zones turned infatuation into missed calls and guilty silences. Three months later, they ended things on a video chat, still kind, still glowing at each other, but clear.

When friends ask now, Mateo calls Harper "the lightning strike that taught me about weather." He says the spark was real, but so was the timing. Harper, journaling from a café in Porto, writes: "Love isn't proof you're ready. Readiness is proof you can love."

They don't regret the heat, only the belief that heat alone could hold them. Both say they would choose it again, but next time, they'll select themselves first, so the timing and the chemistry can arrive together.

Reflection

When has strong chemistry led you astray, and what did you learn?

We reach not just for the other, but for the safety we've always hoped love would bring.

Chapter 5: Attachment – The Invisible Script

How our emotional wiring shapes the way we love, and how to change the patterns that hold us back.

Introduction

Most of us think we choose our relationships based on logic, preference, or shared interests. But beneath those conscious choices is something more profound, an invisible emotional script we began writing long before we started dating, long before we even understood what love meant. That script is our attachment style.

Our attachment patterns are shaped in childhood, but they echo into every adult relationship. They explain why some people seem to need constant reassurance while others pull away the moment things get close. They help us understand the push and pull that so many of us experience but don't know how to name. In this chapter, we'll uncover the roots of attachment, explore the ways it plays out in real life, and talk about how to grow beyond old patterns into more secure, nourishing love.

The Blueprint We Didn't Know We Had

It starts early, long before we know what attachment even means. As infants, we cry out, and someone comes. Or they don't. Or they come inconsistently, unpredictably, lovingly one day and distracted the next. And without realizing it, our nervous systems begin to learn the rules of connection: what love feels like, how safe it is, and whether or not our needs will be met.

Those early lessons form what psychologists call our attachment style. There are several general categories: secure, anxious, avoidant, and a combination called disorganized. These aren't labels to box us in, they're maps. They help us understand the unconscious strategies we use to get close to others or to protect ourselves from being hurt.

Someone with a secure attachment style learned, early on, that love is consistent. That they can trust others to show up, they don't panic at silence or distance, and they're comfortable giving and receiving affection. Those with an anxious style learned that love is inconsistent. They may become hyper, attuned to others' moods, constantly scanning for signs of rejection. They might feel clingy or overly sensitive, not because they want to be, but because love never felt guaranteed. Those with avoidant attachment learned that closeness can be overwhelming or unsafe. They often value independence above all else and may shut down when emotional intensity rises.

These patterns aren't chosen. They're inherited through experience. But here's what's powerful: they're also changeable. Awareness is the first step toward rewriting the script.

Why We Repeat What Hurts Us

One of the more painful realities of attachment is that we often recreate the very dynamics that caused us harm. It's not because we enjoy suffering. It's because, on some deep level, the familiar feels safe, even when it's not.

If you grew up in a household where love was unpredictable, your nervous system learned to live on high alert. As an adult, you might unconsciously gravitate toward people who give you that same push-pull dynamic, not because it feels good, but because it feels known. If love meant working hard to earn attention, you might find yourself overextending in relationships, believing you must prove your worth to be loved at all.

Avoidant patterns repeat, too. If closeness once came with pressure, guilt, or pain, then emotional intimacy may feel suffocating, even when it's kind. You might crave connection but feel repelled by it in real time. You might sabotage relationships before they get too serious, telling yourself you need space, not realizing it's the vulnerability that feels threatening.

These cycles are frustrating. They make us feel stuck. We wonder why we keep ending up in the same dynamic, with different faces. But the reason is simple: we're trying, unconsciously, to resolve the original story. To win the affection we didn't get. To finally feel safe where we once felt abandoned.

The problem is, when we repeat the pattern with someone who can't give us what we need, we only deepen the wound. Healing comes not from reenactment, but from creating something new from choosing relationships where safety is absolute, not earned.

Becoming Secure, Even If You Didn't Start That Way

The best news about attachment is that it's not a life sentence. You may have grown up anxious, avoidant, or disorganized, but you can become more secure. Not by erasing your history, but by responding to it differently. By building new experiences of connection that teach your nervous system a new story.

This process is called "earned secure attachment," and it often begins with awareness. Naming your patterns is like turning on the lights in a room you've always stumbled through. Suddenly, you understand why you panic when someone pulls away, why silence feels like rejection, and why you feel the need to bolt when someone gets too close.

From there, change happens through new experiences. A partner who is calm when you expect chaos. A friend who listens when you anticipate judgment. A therapist who stays grounded when you bring big emotions into the room. Every time someone shows up in a way that challenges your old expectations, your system learns to trust something new.

You also start to appear differently. You learn to soothe your anxiety without demanding reassurance. To stay present during discomfort. To communicate your needs instead of hiding or exploding. These are skills that are learnable, buildable, imperfect, yet powerful.

Becoming securely attached isn't about becoming perfect. It's about becoming real. Honest with yourself. Able to love and be loved without needing the other person to complete you or protect you from your past. Secure attachment isn't the end of conflict or confusion; it's the beginning of resilience, of knowing that no matter what happens, you will not abandon yourself.

Case Study: Ava and the Echo

Ava had always described herself as "clingy", a word she said with a smile, but one that weighed heavily on her relationships. Her last partner called her needy. The one before that was dramatic. But it wasn't until therapy that Ava realized her reactions weren't excessive; they were echoes.

She had grown up with a mother who was present but unpredictable. Some days are warm and affectionate. Other days distracted, distant. Ava never knew which version she would get, and so she learned to scan, to soothe, to pursue.

In adulthood, this translated into anxious attachment. If her partner took too long to respond, she spiraled. If they needed space, she panicked. It wasn't about control; it was about survival.

Once she understood this pattern, Ava stopped blaming herself. She stopped trying to "fix" her attachment style and began responding to it with compassion. Her healing didn't come from a partner fixing her, but from choosing a partner who didn't punish her for needing closeness. Who didn't disappear when things got hard. Over time, she rewrote the script, not by erasing her past, but by loving herself through it.

Reflection

Which attachment pattern most resonates with your behavior?

Sometimes, the loudest silence is the one between words left unsaid, and the ears no longer trying to hear them.

Chapter 6: Communication or the Lack Thereof

How we speak, how we listen, and what happens when we stop doing either well.

Introduction

Most relationships don't fall apart because of a single catastrophic event. They erode quietly, through miscommunications, assumptions, missed signals, and words that go unspoken. It's not that people stop loving each other. The problem is that they stop understanding each other.

Communication is the connective tissue of every relationship. It's how we express needs, process conflict, offer affection, and create meaning together. But it's also one of the easiest things to get wrong. This chapter explores the gap between what we say and what we mean, the ways we mishear those we love, and how learning to communicate with clarity, curiosity, and courage can radically shift the quality of our relationships.

Speaking Without Saying Much

There's a moment in every long-term relationship when you think you're being clear, and the other person hears something entirely different. You say, "I'm fine," and they hear a green light. You meant, "I'm exhausted and overwhelmed, and I need you to notice." They miss it. Not because they don't care. But because they can't read your mind.

We all do this. We hope the people closest to us will "just know." That they'll pick up on the sigh, the pause, the subtext, and when they don't, we feel hurt, not just by the misunderstanding, but by what we interpret it to mean: They're not paying attention. They don't love me enough. I shouldn't have to ask.

But the truth is, clarity isn't selfish; it's loving. When we don't say what we mean, we invite misinterpretation. We confuse silence for strength and subtlety for emotional intelligence. And in doing so, we deprive ourselves of the connection we crave.

Many of us learned early on that asking for what we need made us difficult. That expressing hurt would lead to conflict. So we developed the habit of saying less than we feel. We hint. We imply. We expect others to decode us.

Yet the healthiest relationships aren't built on unspoken understanding, they're built on courageous clarity. On naming emotions before they explode. On saying "I'm struggling right now and I need a little care" instead of hoping someone will figure it out. Speaking honestly doesn't make you needy. It makes you trustworthy. It gives the people who love you a fair chance to love you well.

Listening Without Really Hearing

If speaking honestly is half the equation, listening well is the other half, and it's just as tricky. We often think we're listening when we're waiting for our turn to talk. We hear the words, but not the emotion behind them. We usually respond to what someone said, rather than what they meant.

Real listening is an act of presence. It means putting aside our agenda for a moment, our need to fix, explain, or defend, and letting the other person's experience matter. It means being more curious than correct.

In intimate relationships, especially, this kind of listening can be uncomfortable. When someone we love expresses pain, we want to make it stop. We rush to solutions. We explain our side. We try to justify the thing that hurt them because we didn't mean for it to break. But in doing so, we often make things worse.

What most people want, what we all want, is to be understood and not corrected and not dismissed and not hurried toward resolution. Just understood. When someone says, "I felt alone when you didn't respond," they're not asking for a technical explanation of why you didn't text back. They're asking, "Do you see me? Do you care how I feel?"

The best listeners are the ones who create space for someone else's truth, even when it's hard to hear. They don't always agree. But they stay. They hold eye contact. They say, "I get it," or "Tell me more." And in doing so, they build the kind of trust that makes everything else —repair, intimacy, love —possible.

When Silence Becomes a Language

Not all communication happens through words. Sometimes, the most important messages are sent through silence. The long pause after a question. The turning away in bed. The distracted replies. These moments say something, even when nothing is being said.

Silence isn't always avoidance. Sometimes it's protection. We fall silent because we don't feel safe speaking. Because we've been punished for expressing too much. Or because we're afraid of what will happen if we say what we think. But over time, silence stops being protective and starts becoming corrosive.

In a relationship, chronic silence can become a language of its own, one that says, "We don't talk about that here." And slowly, a wall builds, not from one moment, but from the accumulation of unsaid things. Resentments grow roots. Assumptions become facts. Intimacy fades.

Breaking that silence isn't easy. It often feels like picking at a wound. But the cost of avoiding it is far greater. Unspoken truths don't go away. They live under the surface, shaping our reactions, our moods, even our bodies. They show up in tension, in distance, in explosions over small things.

The path forward is slow but simple: one honest sentence. One open-ended question. One conversation where both people agree to stay curious, even if they're uncomfortable. The goal isn't perfect communication, it's presence. The willingness to say, "This matters. Let's try."

Because the opposite of silence isn't shouting, it's understanding. And once that begins, even the most brutal truths become easier to hold.

Case Study: Priya and the Pause

Priya and Matt had been together for four years. From the outside, they looked solid. They rarely fought, never raised their voices, and always showed up for each other's milestones. But something had started to shift.

It wasn't a blow-up. It was the silence between sentences. The way Priya would say, "I just feel off lately," and Matt would respond with solutions instead of curiosity. Or how Matt would retreat to his office after work, headphones on, leaving Priya to wonder whether he was tired or just tired of *her*.

They didn't fight because neither of them felt safe enough to say what they meant. Priya feared being "too emotional," a label she'd worn since childhood. Matt feared conflict, period; he'd grown up in a household where arguments turned violent. So when tension appeared, he shut down. She tried harder. He withdrew more.

One night, over dinner, Priya said, "I don't feel close to you anymore." Matt looked up, startled. "What are you talking about? I'm here every night."

That was the moment she realized he didn't hear her, not really.

The following week, she brought up the idea of couples therapy. Matt shrugged. "If we need therapy, we're already in trouble."

They never went.

Six months later, Priya ended things, not because she stopped loving him, but because she felt invisible in his presence. "It's not that you don't talk to me," she said. "It's that you don't listen when I try."

Years later, Matt told a mutual friend, "I thought we were fine. I didn't know silence could be so loud."

Priya now describes that relationship as "quietly devastating." Not because it was dramatic, but because of everything they didn't say. What she's learned since: love doesn't mean never arguing. It means caring enough to risk honesty. It means asking better questions, listening without fixing, and speaking without fear of being too much.

She's dating someone new now. It's messier, more honest. And when things get hard, she doesn't pause and retreat; she leans in.

Reflection

What's one need you've never clearly expressed, and why?

True intimacy begins the moment we let ourselves be seen, not as perfect, but as real.

Chapter 7: The Power of Vulnerability

Why intimacy is terrifying, and how to show up fully without losing yourself in the process.

Introduction

We crave closeness, but we fear it too. We want to be truly seen, but when someone gets too close, we flinch. Vulnerability, the heart of intimacy, is often mistaken for weakness. In reality, it's the most courageous act in any relationship: to let someone see the parts of you that aren't polished, aren't protected, aren't perfectly under control.

This chapter explores what it means to be vulnerable, not performatively, but authentically. We'll look at the fear beneath the armor we wear, the walls we build to feel safe, and the moments when we dare to drop the act. Because vulnerability isn't just about disclosure, it's about presence. It's about risk. And it's the only way love becomes real.

The Armor We Learn to Wear

Somewhere along the line, most of us learned that being too open was dangerous. Maybe it was the time we admitted our feelings and were laughed at. Or when we asked for help and were ignored. Perhaps it happened slowly, over the years, little messages that said: Keep it together. Don't be too much. Don't let them see you bleed.

So, we built armor. We became sarcastic instead of sincere. We stayed busy instead of reflective. We polished our stories to control how others saw us. We decided it was safer to be admired than to be known.

The problem with armor, though, is that it doesn't just keep pain out. It keeps the connection out, too. You can't selectively block emotion. When you numb yourself to rejection, you also numb yourself to joy. When you hide your flaws to avoid judgment, you also hide your needs, your depth, your humanity.

This armor shows up in relationships in subtle ways. The joke that covers up hurt. The brush-off when someone offers care. The retreat into silence when something feels too raw. We think we're protecting ourselves, but we're just creating distance, distance from others, and distance from our truth.

Vulnerability doesn't mean oversharing or performing weakness. It means letting down the drawbridge just enough to let someone walk in. It means saying, "This is who I am, even if it scares me. I hope you'll stay."

The Risk of Being Seen

To be vulnerable is to risk. It might not be well-received. To let someone hold your sadness when you're not sure they know what to do with it. To ask, "Do you love me still, even now?" and wait for the answer.

This risk is what makes vulnerability so powerful and so complex. When we reveal our inner world, we give someone the power to reject us. And for many people, especially those who've been hurt before, that feels unbearable. The idea of being open and not received, of being authentic and misunderstood, is enough to keep the walls up forever.

But here's the paradox: without that risk, there's no intimacy. You can build a relationship on charm, intellect, or a surface-level connection. But without vulnerability, it stays thin. Predictable. Safe. And eventually, distant.

The most profound moments of connection, the ones we remember, the ones that shift us, are almost always vulnerable. The moment you cry in front of someone for the first time—the admission of fear. The unguarded laugh, the quiet confession, and the "I love you" were all said first.

These are the moments when we stop performing and start existing. And yes, they're risky. But they're also the only way someone can truly love you, for you, not just for the version you've curated.

And when that love is returned, when someone sees your whole self and stays anyway, it changes everything. It makes the risk worth it.

Staying Open Without Losing Yourself

One of the biggest fears around vulnerability is that it will cost us our autonomy. That, in opening up, we'll become dependent. If we let someone get too close, we'll disappear.

This fear isn't irrational. Many of us have had relationships where being vulnerable meant being manipulated, where our openness was used against us. Where care became control. And so we learn to associate vulnerability with danger, with losing power, with being less ourselves.

But actual vulnerability is not about collapsing into someone. It's about standing firm and saying, "I trust myself enough to let you see me." It's not about abandoning your boundaries; it's about sharing your truth within them. The strongest relationships aren't those where two people merge into one; they're those where both people remain whole, while allowing themselves to be deeply affected by each other.

You can be open and still say no. You can be emotionally available and still protect your peace. You can cry in someone's arms and still be your anchor.

The key is differentiation: the ability to be close without losing your identity. To let someone's experience move you without making it your own. To hold space for their needs without forgetting yours. Vulnerability without boundaries is self-sacrifice. But vulnerability with boundaries? That's love with backbone.

When you find the balance, when you stay soft without going shapeless, you create a connection that's both honest and sustainable. A relationship where love isn't a trade or a trap, but a shared space where two whole selves can meet, again and again.

Case Study: Sam and the Unsent Text

Sam had always been the strong one. One friend came to me in crisis. The one who could calm any storm, keep a level head, and offer advice without blinking. It made them feel useful. Needed. Safe.

But in romantic relationships, that strength became a shield. Sam kept things light, funny, and clever. If someone asked how they were doing emotionally, they'd deflect: "You know me, I'm good." They rarely cried. Never admitted when they felt insecure or afraid. Vulnerability felt like exposure. And exposure had never ended well.

Then they met Riley.

Riley was direct in a way Sam wasn't used to, emotionally fluent, open about needs, quick to say "That hurt," or "I want more from you." At first, Sam admired it. Then resented it. Then, I feared it.

The turning point came after a minor, seemingly insignificant conflict, an unanswered text, and a delayed call. Riley said, "When you disappear emotionally, it makes me feel like I'm the only one in this." Sam wanted to defend themselves, to say it wasn't that deep, to retreat behind logic. But something in Riley's voice, soft, not accusatory, cracked the armor.

Later that night, Sam typed a long message. It explained their walls. Their childhood. They fear being "too much" if they ever ask for help. But they didn't send it.

For hours, they stared at the screen.

Eventually, they pressed send.

And Riley didn't run. They replied, "Thank you. That's the first time I've felt like I met *all* of you."

That moment didn't fix everything. But it opened a door. Sam started speaking from the places they'd always hidden, slowly, sometimes shakily, but honestly. They learned that vulnerability wasn't weakness. It was present. And presence was what made love feel real.

Today, Sam still flinches when emotions rise too fast. But now they pause, breathe, and say, "This feels scary, but I want to stay." And Riley always answers, "Then I'm staying too."

Reflection

Where do you wear emotional armor, and what would it feel like to remove it?

Boundaries aren't walls to keep people out; they're doors that open when it's safe and close when it's not.

Chapter 8: Boundaries – The Bridge and the Wall

How to protect your sense of self without closing the door on connection.

Introduction

We often talk about boundaries like they're barriers, hard lines meant to keep people out. But the truth is, boundaries aren't walls. They're bridges. They help us connect more honestly by defining where we end and where someone else begins. Without boundaries, intimacy becomes enmeshment. With too many, it becomes isolation.

This chapter explores the nuanced role of boundaries in relationships, how they serve not to push people away, but to protect what's most sacred within us. Boundaries aren't about control. They're about clarity. And learning how to set them, hold them, and honor those of others can mean the difference between a connection that drains you and one that helps you grow.

What's Yours and What's Theirs

In the closeness of any relationship, it can be easy to blur the lines between your emotions and someone else's. You feel responsible for their moods. Their silence becomes your fault.

Their stress becomes your burden. Before long, you're not sure where you end and they begin.

This is the first role of a boundary: not to create distance, but to create definition. It says, "I will care about your feelings, but I will not own them." It says, "I can sit with you in your pain, but I cannot fix it for you." It allows us to stay present without being consumed.

Without these lines, love becomes a kind of emotional fusion. We lose our footing. We overextend. We take on guilt that doesn't belong to us or expect others to soothe our anxieties; we need to hold ourselves. It's a subtle erosion, but over time, it leaves both people feeling overwhelmed and unseen.

Healthy boundaries start with self-awareness. What drains you? What restores you? Where do you feel overrun? Where do you tend to disappear? The answers to those questions form the basis of your limits, not as rules to impose on others, but as truths to protect within yourself.

Because when you know what's yours to carry and what isn't, you can show up more fully. You stop managing someone else's emotions and start relating to them. You stop rescuing and start respecting. And that's where real connection begins.

Saying No Without Losing Love

For many of us, saying no doesn't feel like a boundary; it feels like a betrayal. We've been taught, often in subtle ways, that love means selflessness. That care implies compliance. That to turn someone down, to set a limit, to choose ourselves even once, is to risk rejection.

And so we say yes when we're tired. We say "it's fine" when it's not. We make ourselves endlessly available, quietly hoping the people around us will sense our limits and back off before we have to draw a line. But that rarely happens.

What does happen is resentment. Bitterness. Burnout. And confusion, when the very people we wanted to stay close to begin to feel like pressure rather than connection.

Here's the truth: No is not a rejection of love. It's a shape that love can take. A "no" can say, "I care about you enough to be honest." It can say, "I value our connection, and I want to preserve it by not pretending." When we say no with kindness, we build trust. We teach others that our yes is real, not performative.

The fear that people will leave when we set boundaries is not unfounded, but it's clarifying. People who only love you when you're at your best, abandoning you when you're not, were never truly loving *you*. And the people who can hear your no without punishing you for it? Those are the ones who deserve your yes.

Boundaries don't ruin relationships. They reveal them.

Respecting Other People's Boundaries

It's one thing to set your boundaries. It's another thing to respect someone else's, especially when their limits brush up against your desires.

You want to talk things through, and they need space. You're ready to move forward, and they ask for time. You reach for closeness, and they say, "Not yet." In those moments, it's easy to feel rejected. It's tempting to push. To explain. To make your case. But honoring a boundary means listening not for agreement, but for understanding.

This doesn't mean you suppress your own needs. It means you learn to hold the difference between yours and theirs with grace. You say, "I feel hurt, but I won't try to override your limit." You say, "This is hard for me, but I respect what you're asking." You resist the urge to take their boundary personally, and in doing so, you create a space where both people are allowed to be whole.

When we ignore someone's limits, even out of love, we erode trust. But when we honor them, even when we're frustrated, we build it. We show that our love doesn't demand access. It can handle a closed door. That it can wait, adjust, soften.

Because in the end, the relationships that last are not the ones where no boundaries exist. They're the ones where boundaries are respected, early, often, and with care.

Case Study: Nina and the Disappearing Line

Nina had always thought of herself as easygoing. Adaptable. Low maintenance. The kind of partner who "didn't need much." And in every relationship, she played the same role: the giver.

When her boyfriend, Leo, wanted space, she gave it, without asking if she needed closeness. When he missed plans, she said, "It's fine." When he forgot her birthday, she told herself, "He's just not good with dates." She rarely asked for anything that might make her feel "too demanding."

At first, Leo appreciated her flexibility. But over time, a quiet tension built beneath the surface, and Nina started resenting him, not for what he did, but for what *she didn't say*. She felt invisible in her relationship and began pulling back in small ways. Short replies. Less eye contact. I'm going along with the plans, but I feel checked out.

One night, after he'd cancelled yet another dinner to work late, Nina snapped, not with anger, but with clarity. "I don't feel like I exist in this relationship unless I'm accommodating you," she said. "And that's not your fault. It's mine. I trained you not to expect me to have needs."

It was the first time she'd said something like that out loud. And it terrified her.

Leo didn't know what to say. He looked stunned. But instead of defending himself, he asked, "What do you need now?"

The answer surprised her.

"I need to learn how to be disappointing," she said. "Because I've spent my whole life trying not to be. And it's made me disappear."

From that day forward, Nina started practicing boundaries, first in small ways. She said no to last-minute plan changes. She asked to talk through misalignments instead of brushing them off. And every time Leo respected her boundary, she felt safer, not just with him, but with herself.

They're still together. And Leo still isn't great with birthdays. But now, Nina reminds him early. And when he shows up, she doesn't just feel celebrated, she feels *real*.

Because she learned that boundaries aren't ultimatums, they're invitations to meet her, fully. And for the first time, she believes she's worthy of that meeting.

Reflection

Name a boundary you struggle to set, and one you'd like to test.

You didn't write the first chapters, but you get to choose how the story continues.

Chapter 9: The Stories We Carry

How emotional inheritance shapes our view of love, and how to stop living out someone else's script.

Introduction

Every relationship we enter is shaped, in part, by the ones that came before it. Not just our past relationships, but the ones we watched, absorbed, and internalized long before we knew what love even meant. The ways our parents spoke to each other. The silent tensions. The dramas we witnessed. The affection we saw or didn't. All of it leaves an imprint.

This chapter explores the concept of emotional inheritance: the unspoken, often unconscious stories we carry about what love should feel like, how conflict plays out, who we need to be to be loved, and what we're allowed to want. These stories aren't facts, but until we examine them, we treat them like they are. And in doing so, we risk repeating the very patterns we swore we'd avoid.

Inheriting What Was Never Ours

You didn't choose the way your family loved or didn't love. But it shaped you all the same. Perhaps you've seen your parents avoid each other for years, learning that silence is safer than conflict. Maybe you've seen affection weaponized, leading you to believe that love is a performance, something you have to earn. Or maybe love in your home was chaotic, passionate, but unstable, and now anything calm feels boring.

These lessons weren't formal. They were absorbed through dinner table glances, slammed doors, the way people apologized or didn't. And over time, they became your default setting. The lens through which you interpret intimacy.

So now, when a partner pulls away for space, you panic, not because of the present moment, but because it activates an old wound. Or you shut down in arguments, not because you don't care, but because you learned that speaking up makes everything worse. You carry these reflexes like heirlooms, not realizing they were never really yours.

It's not about blaming your family. It's about understanding your wiring. Once you name these inherited patterns, they lose their grip. They stop feeling like universal truths and start becoming what they are: choices you get to make now, consciously, instead of reenacting them on repeat.

The Role We Played, and Still Play

Families, like any long-running story, assign roles. There's the golden child. The fixer. The caretaker. The rebel. The quiet one. The peacemaker. You may have played more than one or moved between them, depending on who needed what.

These roles helped you survive. They gave you identity, predictability, and sometimes even protection. But they also boxed you in. They told you what emotions were acceptable, what needs were allowed, and who you were expected to be about others.

And without realizing it, you may still be playing the same role now. The partner who always holds everything together. The friend who listens but never shares. The one who keeps the peace at the expense of truth. You may enter relationships already shaped by who you think you're supposed to be, not who you are.

This isn't a weakness. It's muscle memory. But when we unconsciously bring old roles into new relationships, we limit the intimacy we can create. We're not showing up fully; we're showing up rehearsed.

The work is in loosening the script. In noticing when you're reacting out of habit rather than intention. In asking: "Is this me, or is this who I learned to be?" And in permitting yourself to be something else.

Because love doesn't require you to stay in character, it asks you to be real.

Rewriting the Narrative

The most liberating moment in any relationship is the one where you realize: I don't have to keep repeating this. I don't have to play out the same argument my parents had. I don't have to choose someone who reminds me of the people who hurt me. I don't have to be the version of myself I've always been. I can choose differently.

But change doesn't start with the other person. It starts inside. It begins when you notice the old story, "I'm too much," "Love always leaves," "I have to earn my worth", and say, "Maybe that's not true anymore."

You begin by telling the truth. Not the one you've inherited, but the one you're discovering. You speak it in therapy. In journaling. In conversation with someone safe. You name what was missing, what you still long for, what you've been pretending doesn't hurt.

And then you practice love in a new way. You stay when you want to run. You soften when you want to armor up. You set a boundary, even if your voice shakes. You let someone care for you without proving yourself first. It won't feel natural at first. That's okay. New stories always feel strange before they feel true.

But with time, repetition, and courage, you build something different. A relationship not built on inheritance, but on intention. Not a reenactment, but a rewrite.

Case Study: Malik and the Silent Contract

Malik didn't think much about his parents' relationship growing up. It was quiet, routine, predictable. His mother ran the house like a CEO, organized, competent, and composed. His father was distant but dependable, always there but rarely *present*. They rarely fought. But they seldom laughed either.

To Malik, this seemed normal.

So, when he started dating Hana in his early 30s, he was confused by her emotional intensity. She wanted to talk, really talk, about feelings, fears, dreams. She asked deep questions. She cried easily. She also challenged him when he shut down, saying, "I feel like I'm loving someone who's standing behind glass."

Malik didn't understand. He was kind. Loyal. He showed up, paid attention, and never yelled. But he had a hard time *responding* to emotion, to conflict, to intimacy. When Hana would say, "Tell me what you need," Malik would freeze. He didn't know.

One night, after an argument that ended in her tears and his silence, Hana said gently, "I think you learned how to disappear with your eyes open."

That line haunted him.

He started noticing the ways he kept himself small in relationships. How uncomfortable vulnerability felt. How much he feared being seen not because he had something to hide, but because he had no idea what lived underneath.

In therapy, he began tracing the shape of his emotional story. He realized he'd inherited more than his father's quiet demeanor; he'd inherited a belief that emotional safety was built on avoidance, not engagement. That if he didn't make waves, no one would leave.

But Hana didn't want quiet compliance. She wanted the *truth*.

The turning point wasn't dramatic. It came one morning when Malik said, unprompted, "I don't know how to share my feelings. But I want to learn." Hana's eyes filled with tears, not because he had figured it out, but because he had stopped pretending.

They're still doing the work. Sometimes, Malik still reaches for old scripts. But now, he pauses and asks himself: *Is this mine? Or is this inherited?*

And with that awareness, he rewrites the following line.

Reflection

Which family story still shapes your expectations of love?

Desire isn't just about heat; it's about honesty, presence, and the courage to be known.

Chapter 10: Sex, Affection, and Desire

What physical intimacy means, why it changes, and how to keep it honest and alive.

Introduction

Sex is often portrayed as the heart of romantic love, passionate, effortless, and ever-present. But in authentic relationships, physical intimacy is more complex. It can be a source of connection, healing, joy, frustration, confusion, and pain. It reflects not just chemistry, but communication, trust, timing, and emotional presence.

This chapter explores what sex and affection mean beyond the surface. We'll look at why desire changes, how physical touch can build or break intimacy, and why keeping the conversation open, even when it's awkward, is the key to sustaining a physical connection that's not just active, but meaningful.

More Than Just a Physical Act

Sex is never just sex. Whether we realize it or not, it carries meaning. It can say, "I see you," or "I need you." It can be an act of love, of escape, of curiosity, of reassurance. It can bring people closer or reveal the distance that already exists between them.

For some, sex is a language, a way to express affection that words can't reach. For others, it's vulnerable territory, tied to fear or shame. How we experience sex is shaped by everything we've ever learned about our bodies, our worth, and our safety. Childhood messages, cultural scripts, and past relationships all show up in the bedroom.

That's why it's so important to approach physical intimacy with care. Not just consent, though that's essential, but attention. What does your partner need to feel safe, desired, and at ease? What do you need? Do you know how to say it out loud?

In healthy relationships, sex isn't a performance. It's a collaboration. A space to be real, to experiment, to feel alive without pressure. It's not about always being in sync but about staying curious when you're not. About asking, "What do you want?" and "What would feel good right now?" and "Is there anything you need that we haven't talked about?"

Affection, whether sexual or not, is a conversation. When we stop talking about it, we stop growing in it. But when we stay open, we build a connection that's not just physical, but profoundly personal.

When Desire Changes

Desire doesn't move in a straight line. It waxes and wanes, softens and spikes. Some days it's a whisper, other days a roar.

And in long-term relationships, it's common for that once electric spark to feel... quieter.

This shift can be terrifying, especially if no one prepared you for it. We're taught to equate desire with newness, urgency, and spontaneity. So when it fades, we assume something's wrong: with us, with our partner, with the relationship itself. But fading desire isn't a failure. It's an invitation.

Over time, what fuels intimacy changes. In the beginning, it's often novelty. Later, it becomes trust, comfort, and depth. But that transition isn't automatic. It requires intention. In the busy middle of careers, kids, stress, and aging bodies, sex can fall off the radar, not because the love is gone, but because life is loud.

That's why desire needs tending. Not pressure, not performance, but attention. Desire grows in presence, in slowness, in moments of play and touch that aren't goal-oriented. It grows when we feel emotionally connected, when we're rested, when we don't feel like we're performing or giving more than we're receiving.

Sometimes, reigniting desire means changing the script: trying something new, laughing during it, pausing for eye contact instead of rushing to the finish. And sometimes it means talking honestly about what's changed, what hurts, what's missing, what's scary to admit.

Because sex isn't about perfection, it's about connection. And connection can always be rebuilt, even after silence, even after distance. It starts with a willingness to look again, gently, and say: "I still want to know you here."

The Affection We Don't Talk About

Not all intimacy is sexual, and not all sexual connection comes from sex. Sometimes, it's in the smallest gestures: a hand on the lower back—a thumb tracing the line of a jaw. A forehead pressed against another's in the dark. These touches don't make headlines, but they say something essential: "I'm here. You matter. You're safe with me."

Affection is the quiet foundation of physical connection. Without it, sex can become transactional, something done rather than something shared. With it, even periods of low sexual activity can still feel deeply bonded. And yet, many couples stop touching outside the bedroom. They stop kissing for no reason. They stop cuddling without expecting more.

Over time, this creates distance. Not because anyone stopped loving, but because they stopped reaching.

We often forget how powerful non, sexual affection can be, how a long hug after a fight can say what words can't. Holding someone's hand in public can create a private world between two people. These moments build trust. They regulate our nervous systems. They remind us that connection is still alive, even when words fail.

If physical affection has faded in your relationship, it doesn't mean it's gone for good. But someone has to go first. A gentle touch. A lingering glance. A small risk of re-injury. Affection doesn't have to be spontaneous to be meaningful; it just has to be offered with care.

Because at its heart, intimacy is presence. And presence can be felt in a kiss, in a touch, in the quiet space between two hands finding each other again.

Case Study: Marcus and the Quiet Reconnection

After fifteen years of marriage, Marcus and his wife hadn't had sex in almost nine months. It wasn't out of anger or infidelity, it was just... life. Two demanding jobs. Teenagers. Sleepless nights. The rhythm of their days had shifted from intimacy to efficiency.

At first, Marcus tried to spark something by planning a romantic weekend. It flopped. They were both exhausted and awkward, which led to an argument. That night, they lay side by side, staring at the ceiling, unsure of what to say.

The next morning, something simple happened: Marcus reached for her hand over coffee. No agenda. No pressure. Just presence.

That one gesture led to a conversation, not about sex, but about closeness. About how unseen they'd both been feeling. About how physical intimacy had become a symbol of more profound disconnection. And from there, they started small. Not with a goal, but with affection. Touch without expectation. Words of appreciation. Eye contact. Laughter.

Desire returned, eventually. But not because they chased it. Because they created the conditions that allowed it to grow.

Reflection

How has your experience of desire shifted over time?

Even silence has a sound when something still matters.

Chapter 11: Conflict as a Doorway

Why arguments aren't a problem, and how to use them as a path to deeper understanding

Introduction

Most of us fear conflict. We associate it with rupture, with losing love, with things falling apart. But what if conflict isn't the end of connection, but the beginning of something more profound? What if arguments, handled well, are not proof of failure but evidence of growth trying to happen?

This chapter looks at conflict not as something to be avoided, but as a doorway to greater intimacy. We'll explore why we fight, what we're fighting about, and how the way we repair, more than the fact that we argued, determines the strength of the relationship, because real love doesn't mean never disagreeing. It means learning how to disagree without breaking each other in the process.

What We're Fighting About

Most arguments aren't about the thing we say they're about. The dishes are in the sink. The unanswered text. The forgotten anniversary. Those are the sparks, but not the fire. The real fire, the one smoldering beneath, is almost always emotional. It's about feeling unheard, unseen, and unimportant.

You say, "You never help around the house," but what you mean is, "I feel alone in this." You say, "You're always on your phone," but what you're asking is, "Do I matter to you right now?" These deeper needs rarely make it to the surface. Instead, they hide behind blame, sarcasm, withdrawal, or volume.

The trouble is, most of us respond to the content of the argument, not the emotion underneath. We defend ourselves against the accusation instead of inquiring about the source of the wound. We escalate when we feel misunderstood, then retreat when we feel judged. And the more we do this, the more the cycle repeats.

But when we pause long enough to ask, "What's going on here?" everything softens. Suddenly, it's not about the dishes. It's about partnership. It's about feeling like we're in this together. And that's something both people can care about, even if they disagree about the details.

Seeing the argument as a symptom, not the core issue, helps us respond with empathy instead of ego. And that shift, from "winning" to understanding, is what turns conflict into connection.

The Way We Fight Matters More Than Why

Every couple fights. The difference between a healthy relationship and an unhealthy one isn't the presence of conflict; it's the presence of repair. It's how you fight, not just that you do.

In some relationships, conflict is loud. Voices rise, doors slam, emotions spill over. In others, it's quiet, distance, coldness, avoidance. Both can be damaging if they become the default. But in either case, there's an opportunity to shift the dynamic.

Fighting well means staying grounded in the shared goal: to understand, not to dominate. It means using "I" statements instead of accusations. "I felt dismissed when you interrupted me," instead of, "You never listen." It means knowing when to pause, when to breathe, when to say, "Let's come back to this when we're calmer."

Fighting well also means regulating yourself. Your nervous system can't be in fight or flight and expect to have a constructive dialogue. If your heart is pounding, if your jaw is tight, if your voice is shaking, it's okay to say, "I need a moment." That's not avoidance. That's wisdom.

And perhaps most importantly, fighting well means knowing how to come back together. To say, "I'm sorry I hurt you," even if your intention was good. To say, "Help me understand what that felt like for you." To hold the space between two truths, yours and theirs, without needing one to win.

In the end, conflict is inevitable. But how we navigate it determines whether it leaves scars or builds strength. Whether it breaks the connection or deepens it.

The Art of Repair

What makes love last isn't perfection, it's repair. The ability to come back after a rupture, to tend to the wound, to say: "We may have hurt each other, but we're still here."

Repair isn't about erasing what happened. It's about owning it. Saying, "I didn't show up the way I wanted to. I want to try again." It's about recognizing not just your actions, but their impact. Even if you didn't mean to cause harm, if harm was caused, it matters.

A sincere repair is specific. It doesn't rush. It doesn't say, "I'm sorry you feel that way," which can sound like dismissal wrapped in politeness. It says, "I'm sorry I said that. I see how it hurt you." It also doesn't demand instant forgiveness. Repair is an offering, not a transaction.

Sometimes, the most challenging part of repair is vulnerability. To admit you were wrong. To hear how your actions affected someone you love. But this is where relationships grow. Not in the flawless moments, but in the imperfect ones, the ones where you stayed. Where you didn't shut down. Where you chose to rebuild instead of retreat.

And when both people learn to do this, to come back to each other after distance, to reach instead of recoil, they build something resilient. A kind of love that's not afraid of stormy weather, because it's learned how to patch the roof.

Case Study: Layla and Ben – The Argument That Opened Everything

Layla and Ben rarely fought in the first year of their relationship. They called it "good communication," but in reality, they were just careful, tiptoeing around disagreements, buffering every frustration with a joke or a shrug.

But as they moved in together, the stakes rose. Suddenly, the sound of toothpaste caps, dishes in the sink, and minor scheduling mishaps felt louder. Still, neither said much. Until one night, a simple miscommunication —Ben forgetting to pick up dinner after promising to —sparked something deeper.

Layla, hungry and exhausted from work, snapped. "You don't listen. You say things and never follow through." Ben, taken aback, fired back: "You act like I'm a screw-up every time I make a mistake. You don't let anything go."

Silence followed. Both of them stood in separate rooms, stunned, not by the volume of the argument, but by how much truth had slipped out in just a few angry sentences.

Later that night, they came back together, tentative, quieter.

Layla spoke first. "It's not about dinner. It's about whether I can trust you with things that matter."

Ben nodded. "And it's not that I don't care. It's that I feel like I'm always being measured and falling short."

That conversation, raw, messy, and unpolished, became their turning point. For the first time, they stopped trying to win or retreat. They stayed. Asked more questions and listened to the answers without getting defensive.

Over time, their fights became less about blame and more about curiosity. They began asking each other, mid-conflict, "What are you really trying to say here?" and "What do you need from me right now?"

They still argue sometimes. But now, conflict feels like a portal, not a danger.

Layla once told a friend, "I used to think love meant avoiding fights. Now I think love is knowing we can fight and find each other on the other side."

Reflection

Think of a recent argument. What was the more profound need underneath?

Some paths wind together. Others diverge. Growth is choosing which direction honors you both, even when the road splits.

Chapter 12: Growing Together (or Apart)

What it means to evolve inside a relationship, and how to know when it's time to let go or lean in.

Introduction

No one stays the same. We grow. We learn. We change our minds, our habits, our priorities. And in a relationship, this means one truth becomes inevitable: the person you started with is not the same person you're with years later. The question isn't whether people change. The question is whether they can change *in relation to* each other.

In this chapter, we explore how to navigate growth inside a relationship, how to support each other's evolution, how to stay connected through seasons of transformation, and how to recognize when growing apart is no longer a threat, but a truth. Because sometimes love adapts. And sometimes, love lets go.

Change Is Not a Betrayal

We often feel afraid when our partner changes, especially if they change in ways we didn't expect. Maybe they will become more ambitious. Or more introverted. Or less interested in the things you once shared. The routines shift. The rhythms feel unfamiliar. And suddenly, you start to wonder: who is this person?

That fear is natural. We build relationships on a foundation of who someone is at a particular moment. When they change, it can feel like they're slipping out of reach. But the truth is, change isn't betrayal. It's biology. It's human. And a relationship isn't supposed to be a time capsule; it's supposed to be a living thing, growing and shifting with the people inside it.

This doesn't mean you have to accept every change without question. It means you have to stay in conversation. Ask what's underneath the shift. Get curious instead of reactive. Say, "I've noticed something's different, tell me about it," instead of, "You're not who you used to be."

Relationships thrive when they allow room for becoming, when change isn't feared but welcomed. When people are allowed to outgrow ideas, habits, even versions of themselves, and remain held.

The couples who last are not the ones who never change; they're the ones who adapt together. Who reintroduce themselves to each other over and over, saying, "This is who I am now, can we keep going from here?"

When One Grows Faster Than the Other

Sometimes, change happens unevenly. One person begins therapy. Starts a new passion. Heals a long-standing wound. And the other? Stays still. Not because they're wrong or unwilling, but because their timing is different. And suddenly, a quiet tension arises.

You begin to speak different emotional languages. The things you used to bond over no longer feel aligned. One person feels inspired. The other feels threatened. One wants to explore. The other wants to preserve. And the gap begins to widen.

This isn't always a crisis, but it is a crossroads. The key is how the difference is handled. Is the growing person judgmental? Superior? Or do they extend an invitation, "I'm on this path, and I'd love for you to join me when you're ready"? Is the partner who's not growing defensive? Resistant? Or simply moving at a different pace?

Growth doesn't always happen in sync. But relationships can withstand that as long as both people are willing to *stay connected* while moving at different speeds. That connection might look like asking questions and listening without defensiveness and encouraging without pushing.

But when the distance becomes too great, when curiosity is replaced by criticism, or when one person's evolution threatens the very foundation of the relationship, sometimes the most honest thing you can do is ask, "Is this still working for who we are now?"

Not out of blame. Out of respect. For yourself, for the other person, and for the journey you've shared.

Staying, Leaving, or Reimagining

Not every relationship is meant to last forever. Some serve a purpose, teach a lesson, or reflect a version of us that no longer fits. And yet, leaving is rarely easy even when the connection feels stagnant. Even when the growth feels one-sided. There's history. There's hope. There's fear of the unknown.

But staying by default, out of comfort or obligation, is not the same as staying by choice. A relationship that lasts out of inertia may not be a relationship at all; it may be a shared routine, a habit, a contract no one wants to renegotiate.

The real question isn't, "Should we stay together?" It's, "Can we continue to choose each other *as we are now*?" Can we reimagine this relationship in a way that honors who we're both becoming? Sometimes that means recommitting and starting fresh within the same container, making new agreements, and finding joy again.

And sometimes it means letting go. Not as failure, but as a recognition that the chapter has ended. The person you've become no longer fits the life you once shared. The most loving act is to set each other free.

Either way, growth is not the enemy of love. It's the evidence of it. Because to love someone deeply is to want them to become more of who they are, even if that eventually leads them away from you.

Case Study: Lila and the Letting Go

Lila had been with Jonah since university. They had grown up together, built careers, bought a home, and survived a pandemic. But as the years passed, she felt like she was expanding, and he was shrinking. She was exploring new passions, questioning old beliefs. He was standing still.

They didn't fight, not often. But the space between them grew quieter. Lila would ask deep questions, and Jonah would change the subject. He loved her, he said, but he didn't understand why she needed so much *more.*

One afternoon, sitting across from him at their favorite café, Lila asked herself the most challenging question: *Am I staying because I love him, or because I'm afraid of what leaving would mean?*

Two months later, they ended things. Not with a door slam, but a mutual recognition: the relationship they had was not enough for the people they were becoming.

They still talk sometimes, not out of regret, but out of respect. And Lila says she doesn't miss the comfort, she misses the version of herself she was trying not to outgrow. Let her breathe again.

Reflection

Where have you outgrown a relationship, and how did you respond?

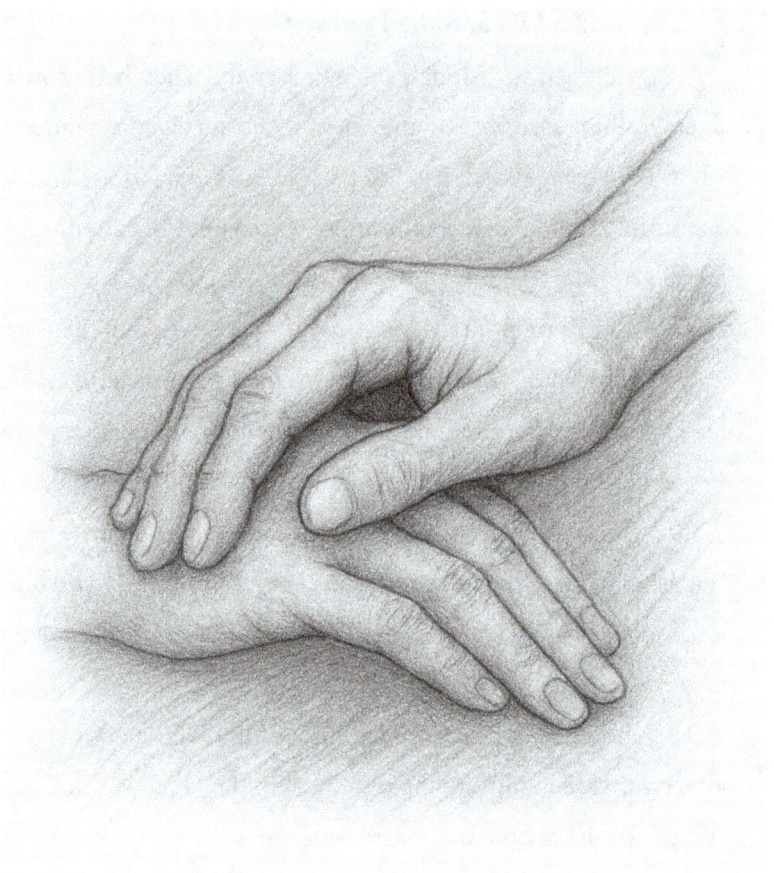

Trust is a bridge we build one step at a time.

Chapter 13: The Role of Trust

How trust is built, how it breaks, and what it takes to rebuild it.

Introduction

Trust isn't built in grand gestures. It's built in small moments, every time someone shows up when they said they would, listens when it would be easier to turn away, and tells the truth even when it's uncomfortable. Trust is the invisible thread that holds relationships together. And when it's intact, everything feels easier. When it's broken, even the smallest interactions feel strained.

In this chapter, we'll explore how trust forms, how it fractures, and what recovery looks like because trust doesn't mean never making mistakes. It means being willing to repair. To show, again and again, that we are safe, honest, and human.

The Slow Build

Trust starts slowly. It doesn't appear with declarations; it builds over time. With consistency. With presence. By noticing the little things. You said you'd call, and you did. You didn't interrupt. You followed through. You admitted you were wrong.

These moments might seem small, but they add up. They become the emotional scaffolding of a relationship. When we trust someone, we don't just believe they won't harm us; we think they'll care when we're hurting, that they'll hold our vulnerability, not exploit it. That they'll tell us the truth, even when it's hard to hear.

And trust isn't just about what the other person does. It's also about what we've experienced in the past. If you've been betrayed, dismissed, or abandoned, you may find it harder to trust, even someone who's never given you a reason to doubt them. Your nervous system remembers. Your guard stays up. Not because you don't want to trust, but because safety has never felt certain.

This is where communication matters. Saying, "I want to trust, but it's hard for me." Saying, "This isn't about you, it's about what I've been through." Letting the other person into the process. Because trust isn't built in silence, it's built in honesty, vulnerability, and time.

When Trust Breaks

There are many ways trust can be broken. Some are obvious: a betrayal, a lie, an affair. Others are subtler but just as damaging: repeated letdowns, emotional distance, promises made and broken. You start to feel like you're walking on eggshells, like the ground underneath you isn't solid anymore.

When trust fractures, everything shifts. The stories we've built begin to unravel. We replay conversations. We question what was real. Sometimes, we don't even know how to ask for what we need; we feel hurt, guarded, unsure.

And the temptation, especially when we've been hurt, is to shut down. To withdraw. To protect. We think, "If I don't let them close, they can't hurt me again." However, this self-protection, while understandable, can also block the path to repair.

Because repair is possible, but only with accountability. Not blame-shifting. Not minimization. Not a rushed, "Can we just move on?" Proper repair begins with acknowledgment: "I hurt you. I broke something. I want to understand how, and I want to rebuild if you'll let me."

It also takes patience. The person who broke trust doesn't get to set the timeline for healing. They don't get to demand forgiveness. All they can do is show up, again and again, with honesty, humility, and consistency.

Rebuilding, If You Choose To

Not every break in trust leads to the end of a relationship. Some ruptures, when met with truth and care, can become the very moments that deepen the bond. But rebuilding trust isn't about pretending the break never happened. It's about creating something new in its place, something more substantial, clearer, more honest.

This process begins with choice. Both people have to want it. The person who was hurt has to decide if they can open the door again. The person who caused harm has to be willing to walk through it with humility.

Then comes the work. Rebuilding trust means transparency, not oversharing, but openness. It means checking in, not out. It means making new agreements, not just recycling old ones. It means asking regularly, "How are we doing? What still feels shaky? What needs more attention?"

It also means tolerating discomfort. Trust doesn't snap back like a rubber band. There will be awkwardness, insecurity, and fear. But with time, effort, and real change, trust can return. And when it does, it's not a return to what was, it's the beginning of something better.

Because trust, once tested, becomes deeper. Not blind but earned. Not assumed, but embodied. And in the process of rebuilding it, you may discover not just each other again, but yourselves.

Case Study: Zoe and the Rebuild

Zoe didn't think of herself as someone with trust issues. She had a close-knit circle of friends, a supportive family, and a steady sense of self. So when she met Eli, charming, thoughtful, present, she let herself lean in quickly. She wasn't guarded. She didn't hesitate.

The beginning was easy. They shared playlists and childhood stories. Spoke often. Laughed freely. There were a few little things that stood out. Eli sometimes took hours to respond to texts or seemed vague about past relationships, but Zoe chalked it up to "being private."

Then, a few months in, she found out, through a mutual acquaintance, that Eli had still been seeing someone else during their first six weeks together. It wasn't technically cheating, Eli explained. They weren't exclusive yet. But to Zoe, it wasn't about the technicalities. It was about the feeling of betrayal, of having trusted something that wasn't fully honest.

She felt her chest tighten every time she thought about their early days. Every sweet memory now carried a hidden clause. She asked herself, "Was anything real?"

Eli apologized immediately, without defensiveness. He didn't minimize what he had done. He didn't beg for forgiveness either. Instead, he said, "If you still want this, I'm ready to do the work. Not to earn you back, but to earn your trust forward."

Zoe didn't rush to decide. She gave herself space to feel angry, betrayed, and unsure. But she also noticed how Eli responded, not just with words, but with consistency. He answered hard questions. He became transparent, not performative. He stopped trying to win her trust back with gestures and started showing up with quiet reliability. No pressure. No urgency. Just presence.

Rebuilding didn't feel romantic. It felt like vulnerability with stakes. Zoe had to learn to listen to her intuition again, not the fear, but the wisdom underneath it. And Eli had to sit with the discomfort of not being entirely trusted, without demanding to be.

Months later, Zoe told a friend, "I'm not sure if things will last forever. But I know this version of us is built on truth, not illusion."

She doesn't use the phrase "forgive and forget." She prefers, "I remember, and I'm watching what's different."

And with that, she rebuilt not just her trust in him, but her confidence in herself.

Reflection

Whom do you trust most, and what small moment built that trust?

Sometimes, the people who know your whole story aren't the ones you fall for, but the ones who stayed.

Chapter 14: Friendship as Foundation

Why romance alone isn't enough, and how the strongest relationships are built on friendship first.

Introduction

Romance burns bright. It's thrilling, intoxicating, full of spark and surprise. But the relationships that last, the ones that weather life's inevitable seasons, aren't fueled by passion alone. They're anchored in something quieter, steadier, and often overlooked: friendship.

This chapter explores how the qualities we value in our closest friends —respect, laughter, forgiveness, shared values, and emotional safety —form the essential foundation for lasting love. Because romance may be what draws us in, but friendship is what helps us stay.

The Overlooked Ingredient

When we think about romantic relationships, we tend to focus on attraction. Chemistry. Intimacy. These things are powerful. But what often gets missed is how essential friendship is to everything else.

Think about your best friend. You probably trust them. You forgive them when they screw up. You laugh together. You support each other's goals. You listen. You don't hold grudges the same way. You allow space for differences. Now imagine bringing those qualities into your romantic relationship, not just when things are good, but especially when they're hard.

Friendship in a romantic partnership means you actually *like* each other beyond desire. You enjoy talking, even when you're not being romantic. You're teammates, not just lovers. It means there's mutual respect; each person values the other's thoughts, contributions, and growth. There's play. There's patience. There's history, built not just on passion, but on presence.

When the early infatuation fades, as it always does, it's friendship that sustains intimacy. Friendship is the soft place you land after a fight. The shared inside jokes. The ease of silence. The knowledge that you're not just partners, you're allies.

Without friendship, even the most passionate relationship starts to feel fragile. With it, love becomes resilient.

When Friendship Fades

Even in relationships that start with a deep friendship, that connection can fade. Life gets busy. Stress piles up. Roles shift, from lovers to co-parents, co-workers, co-survivors. The focus moves from enjoyment to logistics. And before long, the friendship part of the relationship, once so vibrant, begins to disappear.

You stop checking in for fun. Conversations revolve around tasks. You stop laughing at each other's jokes. You assume you already know what the other person thinks. Play becomes rare. Affection becomes duty. And while love may still be there in theory, it no longer feels alive in practice.

This loss can feel subtle but painful. You miss the lightness. The companionship. The feeling that this person is not just your partner, but your friend. Sometimes, this shift happens so gradually that you don't notice it until one of you feels like a stranger.

Rebuilding friendship takes effort, but it doesn't have to be dramatic. It begins with small moments of reconnection. A shared walk. A funny story. A genuine question. A decision to treat each other not just as functionaries in a shared life, but as people worth knowing again.

You don't have to feel "in love" every day. But if you stop nurturing the friendship, you risk losing the very core that made the relationship safe and joyful to begin with.

How to Be Lovers and Friends

Being friends and lovers at the same time requires intention. Passion doesn't always lead to patience. Desire doesn't always include respect. And friendship doesn't always mean chemistry. Balancing both is an art and a practice.

The first piece is presence. Friends show up for each other. They listen. They care about the little things. They ask how you're doing, not just when there's a problem, but because they genuinely want to know. Bringing this level of attention into a romantic relationship keeps the emotional connection alive.

The second is curiosity. Friends stay interested. They don't assume they already know everything. They ask new questions. They let each other evolve. When couples stop being curious about each other, the relationship begins to stagnate. Even after years together, there are still new versions of your partner waiting to be discovered, if you're paying attention.

The third is forgiveness. Friends give grace. They don't keep score. They trust good intentions. In romantic relationships, this kind of forgiveness can be harder, especially when expectations are higher. But when you approach your partner like a friend, instead of a critic, you create space for growth instead of defensiveness.

Lastly, it's about joy. Friends have fun. They're silly. They don't need everything to be productive. Romantic partners sometimes forget this, especially when life feels heavy. But making time to laugh, to play, to *enjoy* each other again? That's what brings the spark back.

Because in the end, passion without friendship burns fast. But love built on friendship? That lasts.

Case Study: Jonah and Cam – The Long Way Around

Jonah met Cam during their first year of college. They shared a study group, a sarcastic sense of humor, and the kind of unspoken ease that made silence feel companionable rather than awkward. Over the next ten years, they watched each other fall in and out of relationships, move cities, try new jobs, fail at some, and cry over more than a few heartbreaks, usually over pizza or long walks.

There was always an undercurrent, something gentle, unspoken. But neither of them pressed it. Cam dated men and women. Jonah mostly dated women. They joked about ending up together "at 40 if we're still single," but they never acted on it. Not because the feeling wasn't there, but because the friendship was too valuable to risk on timing that didn't feel right.

Then, during the pandemic, they ended up back in the same city, both recently single, both a little emotionally threadbare. They started spending more time together, just like before, but something had shifted. It wasn't fireworks. It wasn't heat. It was gravity. Jonah noticed how Cam listened differently now. Cam noticed how Jonah looked at them, less playful, more present.

One night, Jonah said, "I think I've been in love with you for years. I didn't know that's what it was."

Cam didn't respond right away. They sat with it, then replied, "That doesn't scare me. But I want to make sure we're not reaching for each other out of loneliness."

So they didn't rush. They went on a few intentional dates. Talked openly about expectations. Made space for friendship to keep breathing, even as romance bloomed.

Now, three years in, they still check in weekly: *Are we still being friends inside this love?*

They say their foundation isn't passion, though that's grown; it's safety. Ease. The deep knowing that neither of them is trying to be impressive anymore. They're just trying to be present.

Cam likes to say, "We didn't fall in love. We walked there. Slowly. Together."

Reflection

Which qualities in your partner feel most like friendship?

We're in the same room, but not at the exact moment. Presence isn't proximity, it's attention.

Chapter 15: Love in the Digital Age

How modern technology has reshaped dating and connection, and what it means to be truly present with someone.

Introduction

Technology has made it easier than ever to connect, but also harder to feel genuinely connected. We can swipe through hundreds of potential partners in an hour, text someone on the other side of the world in seconds, and share pieces of our lives instantly. But something's changed in the way we relate. We've gained access, but often at the cost of depth.

This chapter explores how digital culture has transformed the way we date, love, ghost, flirt, and stay, or don't. We'll look at the promises and pitfalls of online intimacy, how constant access affects emotional availability, and what it means to truly be present with someone in a world built to distract us.

Swipe Culture and the Illusion of Infinite Choice

The dating world used to be small. You met people through work, school, and mutual friends. You ran into them at a party, a bookstore, or a grocery store. There were limits, and those limits, while frustrating, also created clarity. You gave more people a chance. You stayed longer in conversations. You were more likely to see the whole person instead of filtering them through a checklist of ideal traits.

Now, the world has exploded. You can meet someone with a flick of your finger. If the conversation lags, if the spark isn't immediate, you move on. There's always someone else. Someone potentially more compatible, more attractive, more exciting. You don't have to invest; you have to keep swiping.

At first glance, this feels empowering. More options. More autonomy. But something gets lost in the scroll: depth. Curiosity. Commitment. The understanding that love isn't always instant, it's often built. Dating apps reward snap judgments. They turn people into profiles. And slowly, without even realizing it, we start treating connection like content—something to consume, not cultivate.

This illusion of infinite choice creates what psychologists call "decision fatigue." The more options we have, the less satisfied we tend to be with any one of them. Even when we do meet someone promising, we carry a lingering thought: "Is there someone better just one swipe away?" It's not that we're shallow; it's that the culture teaches us to optimize everything, including love.

But genuine relationships don't work like algorithms. They require time, patience, and the willingness to stay curious when things don't feel perfect. Because perfect doesn't exist, not in real life. Only real does. And real takes time.

Connection vs. Contact

In theory, we've never been more connected. We can FaceTime our partner on a lunch break, send a selfie from the airport, react to each other's stories, and stay in constant digital touch. But in practice, many people feel more alone than ever.

That's because there's a difference between contact and connection. Contact is frequent. Easy. Passive. A quick "hey" or heart emoji. A like. A meme. These things mimic intimacy, but they don't create it. They keep us in each other's orbit without deepening the bond.

Connection, on the other hand, requires intention. It asks for presence. It's not just about updating someone on your day; it's about being emotionally available to *hear* theirs. It's not about sending a text to say "thinking of you", it's about sitting in silence, together, in the same room, and feeling understood.

Digital intimacy can be powerful. Long-distance relationships are sustained by it. Emotional safety can bloom in text threads, in voice notes, in shared playlists, and digital rituals. But it takes effort. And if we're not careful, we begin to confuse digital noise for real closeness.

We often think we're connected because we're in constant contact, but when something real happens, we struggle to be genuinely present. We don't know how to hold space without distractions, without multitasking, without a screen between us.

So, we have to practice. To choose phone calls over texts
sometimes. To put the devices away during dinner. To remember
that real love is less about updates and more about understanding.
Less about presence in the feed, more about presence in the
moment.

Ghosting, Breadcrumbing, and the Fear of Being Too Much

There's a particular kind of pain that comes from being left
without explanation. One minute you're in conversation,
laughing, flirting, maybe even planning a date, and the next,
silence. No fight. No goodbye. Just absence. This is ghosting, and
in the digital age, it has become as common as it is confusing.

Ghosting isn't just about someone disappearing. It's about the
emotional whiplash of it. The way it pulls the rug out from under
our sense of connection. The questions it leaves behind: "Was
any of it real?" "Did I do something wrong?" "Why wasn't I
worth a response?"

And then there's breadcrumbing, the slow, occasional check-
ins that feel like attention but lead nowhere. A heart reaction to
your story. A random text at midnight. A brief spark of hope,
only to be followed by more silence. Breadcrumbing keeps
someone just close enough to feel seen, but never close enough to
feel valued.

These behaviors aren't new, but technology makes them easier to execute and harder to process. In the past, disappearing on someone required courage, confrontation, or at least awkwardness. Now, it requires nothing but indifference and the tap of a screen.

What's most damaging about ghosting and breadcrumbing isn't just the loss of connection; it's the impact on self-worth. It plants the idea that you were "too much." Too needy. Too intense. That if only you'd said less, felt less, asked for less, maybe they would've stayed.

But that's the lie.

The truth is that someone's inability to show up fully says more about their capacity than your worth. Ghosting is often an avoidance of discomfort, not a verdict on your value. It's easier to vanish than to admit fear, disinterest, or unavailability. And breadcrumbing? That's often about control, the desire to feel wanted without offering anything in return.

The antidote to these modern dynamics isn't cynicism. It's clarity. Knowing what you want. Naming your needs and refusing to shrink yourself to keep someone interested. Because the right person won't flinch when you show up honestly, they'll meet you there.

Presence in a World of Distraction

You've probably seen it before: two people sitting across from each other at dinner, each absorbed in their phone. They're together, technically. But they're not *with* each other. And while it's easy to judge from the outside, most of us have been there. Our devices have become extensions of us, always within reach, always pulling our attention away from the moment we're in.

In relationships, this creates a subtle erosion. We miss cues. We respond to tone instead of intention. We forget to make eye contact. Over time, we start feeling unseen, not because the person doesn't care, but because they're not *here*.

Presence is increasingly rare in the digital age. But it's also increasingly powerful. To be fully with someone, to put the phone down, the screen away, the background noise on mute, is an act of love. It says, "Right now, you matter more than anything else." And that kind of attention is healing.

Being present doesn't mean you're always perfectly engaged. It means you notice when you've drifted. You come back. You say, "Sorry, I got distracted. Can you say that again?" It means carving out rituals of undivided attention, such as taking a phone-free walk or a shared breakfast. A few minutes before bed, take a moment to check in not just about logistics, but about feelings.

In a world that constantly fragments our focus, choosing presence becomes a radical act. And the relationships that thrive in this world are the ones where people still look each other in the eye. Still listen with their whole body. Still ask, "What was the best part of your day?" and care about the answer.

Because love doesn't live in updates, it lives in moments. And moments are only real when we show up for them.

Case Study: Theo and the Swipe Spiral

Theo had been on every dating app. Bumble, Hinge, Tinder, Coffee Meets Bagel. He'd gone on more than 40 first dates in a year. Some were decent. Most fizzled. A few were hurt. But more than anything, he felt numb.

Each time he matched with someone new, it gave him a tiny dopamine hit. *Someone wants me.* But the moment it got hard, the moment a conversation stalled, or a feeling of vulnerability rose, he swiped again. Always searching and continuously optimizing. I always wondered if the real connection was just one profile away.

It wasn't until his therapist asked, "What are you afraid you'll feel if you stop swiping?" that Theo realized: it wasn't about finding love. It was about avoiding loneliness. And disappointment. And himself.

He took a break. A real one. Deleted the apps. Started journaling. Started meditating. And only after several months of silence did he feel ready to date again, not from a place of scarcity, but with presence. The first woman he met didn't feel like a fairytale. But she listened. And Theo listened back. And it felt... real. And reality was finally enough.

Reflection

When did digital distraction last pull you away from real presence?

1When difference is met with presence, something new can bloom.

Chapter 16: Love Across Differences

What it takes to connect across lines of race, class, gender, politics, and culture, and why doing so can make love even stronger.

Introduction

We're often drawn to people who feel familiar. Who understands our shorthand? Those who share our background, beliefs, or way of seeing the world. But sometimes, love crosses those lines. We often fall for someone from a different culture. Someone with a different worldview. Someone whose experiences don't mirror ours but challenge them.

These differences can create friction. But they can also create opportunities, opportunities to stretch, to listen, to deepen our understanding of each other and ourselves. This chapter explores what it takes to love across difference, not with blind idealism, but with humility, courage, and the willingness to do the work.

Difference Isn't the Problem, Avoidance Is

When we say, "opposites attract," we usually mean quirks: one's tidy, the other's messy; one's loud, the other's quiet. But what happens when the differences run deeper? Different religious beliefs. Different political identities. Different racial, cultural, or economic backgrounds. These are more than personality traits; they're lenses. They shape how we move through the world, how we define safety, justice, family, and love.

At first, the novelty of these contrasts can be exhilarating. We feel expanded by the unfamiliar. We're intrigued. But eventually, the weight of difference makes itself known, not in the abstract, but in the daily details of how you raise children, how you talk about money. How do you respond to a crisis in the news? Suddenly, it's not just a difference in opinion, it's a difference in *reality*.

This is where many relationships falter, not because of the difference itself, but because of what happens when it's ignored, when people avoid the hard conversations in the name of harmony. When one person consistently adapts, the other tends to stay centered. When curiosity fades and assumptions take over.

Loving across difference requires a different kind of presence. A deeper listening. A willingness to say, "Help me understand what this means to you," and mean it. It's not about erasing difference but honoring it. Saying, "We're not the same, and that's not a threat. That's an invitation."

Power, Privilege, and the Space Between

Some differences are visible. Others are structural. And in any relationship where power imbalances exist, across gender, race, class, or ability, those dynamics don't disappear just because two people love each other. They show up in who gets heard. In whose experiences are centered? In who does the emotional labor, and who takes it for granted.

This can be uncomfortable to talk about, mainly when no harm was intended. But intention isn't the same as impact. And in relationships across lines of privilege, ignoring that impact can lead to profound disconnection.

Consider a scenario where one partner comes from a wealthy background, and the other grew up with financial insecurity. That difference will shape their comfort with spending, their views on debt, and their expectations around work. Or take race, when one partner lives with the daily weight of discrimination, and the other doesn't see it firsthand, it's easy to misread or minimize that pain.

These moments don't mean the relationship is doomed. But they require humility. The willingness to unlearn. To ask, "Where am I missing something?" To resist the reflex to defend or explain and instead sit with discomfort long enough to let it teach you something.

Loving across difference means creating space for both people's truths. It means not expecting your partner to educate you, but still doing the work to educate yourself. It means owning mistakes without collapsing into guilt. Because love without accountability is just sentiment. But love with accountability? That's liberation.

When Values Clash and Conversations Get Hard

There's a difference between preferences and values. Preferences are about taste, music, food, and lifestyle. They can stretch and bend. But values? Those run deeper. They're the moral compass by which we orient our lives. And when two people's values collide, the result isn't just disagreement, it's disorientation.

You believe in open communication; your partner grew up in a culture of emotional restraint. You believe parenting requires emotional validation; they believe in strict discipline. You see political issues as personal; they see them as irrelevant to love. These aren't debates to win, they're realities to navigate.

At first, it might feel easier to avoid these conversations. You tell yourself it's not worth the fight. You compartmentalize. You minimize. But over time, the cracks widen. You begin to feel unseen, or worse, unsafe. You wonder if your core beliefs can coexist. And maybe, in some cases, they can't.

But more often than not, what we need isn't sameness, it's safety. The safety to speak our truth without fear. To say, "This matters to me," and know it won't be dismissed. To disagree without disrespect. To ask, "Can we hold both our values here?" without feeling like one has to disappear.

This kind of emotional safety isn't built in silence. It's built in dialogue, in brave, often messy conversations that don't always end in resolution but do end in understanding. It's built when both people stop trying to win and start trying to *witness*.

Sometimes, you will find a middle ground. Sometimes, you won't. But even when you don't, you can still choose how to love, with compassion, with respect, with curiosity. Because compatibility isn't about perfect agreement, it's about shared willingness. Shared effort. A shared belief that difference doesn't have to mean division.

Building a Shared Language

When you love across difference, you don't just bring your heart. You get your histories. Your vocabulary. Your wounds. And sometimes, the exact words mean very different things. "Love." "Freedom." "Respect." "Tradition." Each person hears them through the filter of their own life.

That's why building a shared language is essential. Not just literally, though in some relationships, language differences are both literal and emotional. It means asking, "When you say that, what do you mean?" It means defining terms. Clarifying intentions. Saying, "This is what that word feels like to me. Does it feel the same to you?"

It also means paying attention to body language, tone, and context. What does silence mean for your partner? Withdrawal? Anger? In one culture, raising your voice is a sign of passion. In another, it's a threat. In one family, physical affection is rare. In another, it's how love is spoken. Without context, these differences can become triggers. With context, they become points of learning.

This process takes time. Patience. Sometimes, translation. But the reward is richer intimacy, because it's earned—a kind of closeness built not on assumed sameness, but on fundamental understanding. When someone takes the time to learn your language, whether spoken, emotional, or cultural, you feel chosen differently.

And when you learn theirs, you say, "I care enough to meet you where you are. Not to change you, but to know you." That's what love across difference requires: not fluency, but effort. Not perfection, but presence. A shared language, slowly built, one conversation at a time.

Case Study: Aisha and Luke

Aisha was raised in a Muslim family in Toronto. Luke grew up Catholic in a small town outside Montreal. They met during a graduate program in international relations, bonded over policy debates, and were surprised to find emotional chemistry layered beneath intellectual respect.

Their first months were electric and complicated. Aisha fasted for Ramadan. Luke attended Easter mass. They didn't push each other, but their differences were unmissable. They joked about it early on, saying, "We'll just celebrate everything," but they both knew faith wasn't just tradition; it was identity.

The more challenging conversations came slowly. How would they raise children, if they had them? Would their families ever understand? Would their love be enough to bridge the weight of expectation?

Aisha remembers the night it shifted. She told Luke, "I'm afraid that love won't be stronger than culture. Or religion. Or the pressure to explain ourselves every time we're in a room together." Luke didn't rush to reassure her. He just said, "Then let's stop trying to explain and start building something they haven't seen before."

They didn't merge beliefs. They made space for both. They read each other's sacred texts. They learned Arabic and French. They created rituals, hybrid, messy, deeply personal, that were wholly their own.

Years later, they still get questions. But they answer less defensively now. Aisha says, "Our relationship doesn't defy tradition; it expands it. We didn't erase the difference to be together. We just stopped letting it divide us."

Reflection

What difference in values or background challenges you, and enriches you?

Love sometimes sounds like two pages turning in unison.

Chapter 17: Family, Children, and the Shifting Center

How relationships evolve when kids arrive, family dynamics change, and priorities shift, and what it takes to stay connected through it all.

Introduction

Love doesn't exist in a vacuum. It lives among the noise of everyday life, career moves, aging parents, growing children, and unexpected crises. And in the thick of all that, the center of the relationship can shift. What once felt like the entire focus, just the two of you, now competes with dozens of new responsibilities and identities.

This chapter explores what happens to relationships when families grow, roles evolve, and life stretches you in every direction. It's not about getting everything right; it's about staying together while everything changes. And about finding your way back to each other, again and again.

When Children Change Everything

Having children is one of the most joyful, disorienting experiences a couple can share. There's awe and tenderness and an overwhelming sense of purpose, but also sleep deprivation, shifting identities, and the unrelenting pressure to be everything to everyone, all at once.

What often gets lost in the middle of it is the relationship that started it all.

In the early years of parenthood, partners can become co-managers, logistics machines handling diapers, daycare, and deadlines. Conversations revolve around needs, schedules, groceries, and meltdowns. Romance takes a backseat, often not out of neglect, but necessity. There's just no energy left at the end of the day for deep connection, let alone intimacy.

And slowly, the gap grows. You start to feel more like roommates than lovers. More like teammates than soulmates. The person you once stayed up all night talking to now shares the bed, but not the emotional landscape.

This shift is standard, but not inevitable. The key is awareness. Recognizing that the relationship needs tending to. That even a ten-minute check is necessary in matters. That a shared laugh while cleaning up dinner is still intimacy, that carving out time, even tiny windows, for each other is not selfish. It's essential.

Because your kids don't just need parents, they need to see a model of love that survives stress. That adapts. That remembers. When they watch you choose each other, especially when it's hard, they learn what love looks like.

The Pull of Extended Family

Families don't disappear when we form new ones. They expand, collide, overlap, and sometimes, create tension. Laws bring their expectations. Siblings need support. Parents grow older and more dependent. And in the middle of it all, your relationship may feel pulled in multiple directions.

You want to set boundaries, but you don't want to offend. You want to be loyal to your partner, but you feel responsible for your family. Holidays become negotiations. Child-rearing decisions become battlegrounds of tradition versus autonomy. And if your partner comes from a very different family culture, these tensions can be magnified.

What's important is not avoiding conflict, it's navigating it with clarity and unity. That means checking in with each other first: "How do *we* want to handle this?" It means making decisions as a team, even when those decisions are hard. It means communicating to extended family not just what you want, but what you *both* need.

Sometimes this requires difficult conversations, saying no to traditions, stepping back from old roles, and defending boundaries others don't understand. But when done with honesty and respect, these boundaries don't divide families. They define the relationship.

And they remind everyone, yourselves included, that your partnership is a home you're building together: one that honors the past, but answers to the present.

Finding Each Other Again After Everything

Even in the strongest relationships, there comes a season when you look across the room at the person you love and think, "We're still here, but we're not quite *us* anymore." It's not always dramatic. Sometimes it's just distance built from survival. The accumulation of long days, short tempers, missed connections, and quiet compromises. You haven't fallen out of love, you've just fallen out of rhythm.

This is common after years of caregiving, whether for children, aging parents, or both. The love is still there, but it's quieter, buried under layers of routine. And the relationship begins to feel less like a garden and more like a hallway, something you pass through without pausing.

But even the most profound connection can be rediscovered. You don't need a grand gesture. What you need is attention. Intention. A willingness to say, "Let's try again."

Start small. Take walks without your phones. Ask each other questions you haven't asked in years. What are you dreaming about now? What's something you miss? What would you change, if you could? Listen with fresh ears. See each other not as co-parents, caregivers, or cohabitants, but as people still becoming.

Make space for joy. Not just the big date nights, but the playful teasing while folding laundry. The spontaneous kiss. The inside joke. These are the threads that reweave the connection.

And when resentment bubbles up, as it sometimes does, don't ignore it. Don't assume time will smooth it out. Talk about what's been hard. What you've needed but didn't know how to ask for. What you're still longing for now.

Because love isn't just something you feel. It's something you return to. Not once, but many times. And every time you find each other again, after the babies, after the burnout, after the chaos, you remember why you chose each other in the first place.

Case Study: Lena and the Living Room

Lena loved Adam deeply. Their relationship felt secure, full of mutual respect, shared humor, and a sense of partnership she hadn't experienced before. But when she first met his family, something in her shifted. Not because they were unkind, but because they were... different.

Adam's family was loud, affectionate, and constantly ribbing each other. They interrupted. They shared everything. They had decades of inside jokes and unspoken dynamics that made Lena feel like an outsider peering through a window. Her upbringing had been quieter, more reserved, structured around politeness and emotional privacy. Every holiday visit left her emotionally exhausted.

She didn't want to make it a problem, but after the third visit, where she came home in tears, she told Adam, "I'm trying to belong, but I feel like I have to lose myself to do it."

Adam listened carefully. He admitted he hadn't noticed how much she was stretching to accommodate his family's energy. "You're always so calm," he said. "I didn't realize how much you were holding in."

That moment became a turning point, not in changing the family dynamic, but in shifting how they approached it *as a team*. Adam started checking in with her before and after visits. Lena began setting limits, stepping outside when she needed space, skipping events that felt performative. She stopped trying to match their volume and started offering her presence in quieter ways, helping in the kitchen, asking thoughtful questions, and finding one-on-one moments with those who seemed open.

And slowly, something shifted not just in how the family saw her, but in how she saw herself within it. She wasn't trying to *become* them anymore. She was allowing herself to *be* herself, with Adam's support.

Now, Lena still doesn't love every family dinner. But she doesn't dread them either. And when they walk in together, hand in hand, she feels grounded, because she knows they're not asking her to erase herself to belong.

Reflection

How has becoming part of a family changed your relationship
dynamics?

Some goodbyes aren't about closure—they're about choosing growth over comfort, and grief over pretending.

Chapter 18: Breakups and Endings

How to end with dignity, grieve with honesty, and grow into your next chapter without bitterness or regret.

Introduction

Some relationships last forever. Many don't. That doesn't mean they failed. It means they served their purpose, for a season, for a lesson, for a version of you that's no longer here. Endings hurt even when they're necessary. Even when they're mutual, they also hold the potential for profound clarity, healing, and rebirth if we allow ourselves to go through the grief instead of around it.

This chapter explores the experience of letting go, not just of the person, but of the story, the dream, the imagined future. It's about closing the door gently, without slamming it, and choosing peace over blame. And about remembering that endings, while painful, are not punishments, they're portals.

The Decision to Leave

There's rarely one moment that makes a breakup inevitable. More often, it's a slow accumulation, a quiet distancing, a pile of unmet needs, a growing ache that something fundamental no longer fits. Maybe you've tried to repair. Perhaps you've stayed longer than you should have. Or maybe you're the one being left, blindsided by a decision you didn't choose.

Whatever your role, the truth is that deciding to end a relationship, especially a long or meaningful one, is rarely clean. Even if you know it's right, there's guilt. Grief. Doubt. You remember the good times. You ask yourself if you tried hard enough. If maybe, just maybe, there's one more thing you could do to fix it.

And sometimes there is. Sometimes the relationship can be renewed with honest work. But sometimes, staying would only prolong the pain. Love alone isn't always enough. If respect has eroded, if trust can't be rebuilt, if the versions of yourselves you've become no longer recognize each other, then staying becomes an act of fear, not of love.

Choosing to leave doesn't mean you didn't love them. It means you also love yourself enough to stop betraying your needs. And being left doesn't mean you weren't worthy. It means that, for reasons beyond your control, the path diverged. You are not a failure. You are a person choosing to honor what's true, even when it hurts.

Grieving What Might Have Been

After a breakup, the hardest part isn't always missing the person. It's missing the *idea* of them. The future you imagined.

The life you were building in your mind. The comfort of knowing where things were going.

There's a unique kind of grief that comes from the loss of potential. You're not just mourning what was; you're mourning what will now never be. The trips you won't take. The home you won't share. The inside jokes that no longer land because the person who understood them is gone.

This grief comes in waves. One day, you feel strong, grounded, and resolute. The next, you're undone by a song, a scent, a random Tuesday afternoon. You wonder if you'll ever feel that connected again. If what you had was your only shot. You replay every conversation, trying to find the exact moment where things went off course.

But grief isn't something to solve. It's something to feel. And if you allow yourself to move through it, without judgment, without shame, you'll find that the pain softens. It doesn't disappear, but it transforms. It becomes part of you. Not a wound, but a scar. A reminder that you dared to love and dared to let go.

Let yourself grieve what might have been. But also stay open to what *could* be, beyond this heartbreak. The future you hadn't planned for yet. The version of you that's just beginning to emerge from the wreckage.

Ending Without Destroying

Breakups are often associated with drama, shouting matches, bitter texts, lines drawn, and friendships divided. That kind of ending can feel cathartic in the moment. But later, it leaves scars. Not just on the relationship, but on the self. Because when we go into destruction, we carry the wreckage with us.

But there's another way.

An ending can be honest without being cruel. It can be clear without being cold. You can say, "This isn't working anymore," without saying, "You never mattered." You can walk away without burning everything behind you.

The key is to resist the temptation to villainize. To make someone bad so you can feel better about leaving. Or to make yourself the sole villain if you're the one being left. Most relationships end not because someone was terrible, but because something between you stopped working. That something deserves compassion, not contempt.

Ending well means acknowledging the love that existed, even if it didn't last. It means offering gratitude for what was real. It means having hard conversations with softness. Saying the words you'll be proud to remember, even if they make you cry now.

If you share a life, children, friends, and a home, ending well also means committing to respect in the aftermath. Do not use your shared history as ammunition. To show up with dignity, especially when it would be easier to lash out.

You won't get it perfect. There may be moments you regret. But if you lead with truth, with care, to do no further harm, you'll walk away clean. And from that place, healing isn't just possible. It's inevitable.

Because how we end things says as much about us as how we begin them. And ending something with kindness? That's not a weakness. That's a strength.

Case Study: Talia and the Gentle Goodbye

Talia had always imagined that if she ever left a relationship, it would be for something dramatic, a betrayal, a breach of trust, a line crossed. But with Jonah, there was no event. No big failure. Just a slow unraveling.

They had been together for five years. On paper, they were a great match. They made each other laugh. Supported each other's careers and loved each other's families. But over time, the conversations became lighter. The affection is more habitual than intentional. They stopped dreaming out loud. Stopped checking in. There was no hostility, just absence.

At first, Talia thought it was a phase. She doubled down, planning a weekend away, starting therapy on her own, and reinitiating physical touch. Jonah went along with it all, kind as ever. But when she finally asked, "Do you feel close to me?" he paused for too long.

"I love you," he said, eventually. "But I don't know if we're growing anymore."

That night, they talked until morning. Not to fix anything, but to tell the truth. About the quiet distance neither of them had named and about the parts of themselves that had changed and about the guilt of letting go of something that wasn't broken, just finished.

They ended the relationship with more tenderness than they had imagined possible. No deleted photos. No harsh words. Just honesty and care.

Talia cried for weeks, not because she regretted leaving, but because it was the first time she had honored her intuition without waiting for things to fall apart. She told a friend, "It wasn't a tragedy. It was a transition. But it still hurt like hell."

Now, when she reflects on that relationship, she doesn't think of it as a failure. She thinks of it as a completed chapter. A season that taught her what companionship can look like, and what self-honoring feels like.

They still talk occasionally. Brief check-ins. A holiday card. A mutual friend's wedding. And every time, she's grateful for the way they ended, with care, not cruelty, because some endings are just that: *a way of loving someone through the goodbye.*

Reflection

What story of "what might have been" do you still carry, and how can you release it?

Love doesn't age out. It deepens, steadies, and holds, especially when everything else changes.

Chapter 19: The Work of Long-Term Love

What it takes to sustain connection over time, and why love that lasts is built, not found.

Introduction

We love the idea of forever. The thought that we might find someone who chooses us, year after year, through every season of life. But what we often overlook is that long-term love isn't just the result of a perfect match. It's the result of ongoing effort.

This chapter is about the work of staying, not staying out of duty or fear, but out of daily, deliberate commitment. It's about what a real, lasting connection requires: not magic, not luck, but maintenance. Because love isn't something you discover once, it's something you create again and again.

Loving the Same Person Over and Over Again

One of the most surprising truths of long-term relationships is that you don't just love one person, you love many versions of them. The twenty, five, year, old with big dreams. The exhausted new parent. The middle-aged partner is grappling with purpose—the older soul who surprises you with softness, or wisdom, or new fears.

And they, in turn, love many versions of you.

This means that staying in love isn't just about holding on. It's about meeting each other anew, again and again. Asking, "Who are you now?" instead of assuming you already know. Letting go of outdated expectations. Allowing your partner to evolve without making their growth feel like a betrayal of who they were.

Too often, we stop seeing our partner as time goes on. We get so used to their presence that we stop being curious. We assume, project, fill in the blanks. And in doing so, we risk losing the dynamic spark that made the relationship feel alive in the first place.

But it doesn't have to fade. You can learn from each other. You can be surprised again. You can notice the new ways they laugh. The new things they care about. The grief they haven't yet named, or the joy they haven't yet shared.

Loving someone for a lifetime isn't about loving them *the same way* forever. It's about loving who they become, and allowing yourself to become with them.

The Myth of Effortless Love

We are surrounded by stories that suggest real love is easy. That if it's right, it flows. That work is a sign of failure. But in truth, *any* lasting relationship involves effort, not because something's wrong, but because people are complex. Needs shift.

Life throws curveballs. Intimacy deepens and contracts. And through it all, love asks to be tended.

The work of long-term love isn't always dramatic. Sometimes, it isn't exciting. It's showing up when you'd rather zone out. It's choosing patience when frustration rises. It's resolving the same fight for the hundredth time, not because you enjoy it, but because you believe the other person is worth understanding.

The effort appears to be focused on initiating repairs following a complicated conversation. Like learning how your partner feels about love now, not ten years ago. Like asking, "How can I support you?" even when you're tired. It's an effort that says: I care not just about how we feel in this moment, but about who we're becoming together.

And yet, effort isn't the same as struggle. There's a difference between the natural work of growing with someone and the exhausting work of constantly justifying your worth. Love should stretch you, not deplete you. It should challenge you, not wound you. When effort becomes survival, when the relationship feels like a job rather than a joy, it's worth asking what kind of "work" you're doing, and why.

The healthiest relationships require effort, but they also reward it. They feel safer, deeper, richer over time. Not because they avoid difficulty, but because they move through it with intention and care.

Ritual, Renewal, and the Small Things That Matter

In the beginning, everything feels like magic. Every text, every glance, every shared secret is electric. But over time, magic fades, not because the relationship is broken, but because the extraordinary becomes ordinary. The person who once made your heart race is now folding laundry beside you. And in that ordinariness, love begins to either quietly deepen or quietly disappear.

The difference lies in how we treat the small things.

Grand gestures don't sustain long-term love. It's sustained by ritual. By the cup of coffee made every morning. By the "text me when you get there." By the goodnight kiss that doesn't feel like a habit, but a promise, these tiny acts aren't filler, they're glue. They remind each person, again and again: I see you. I care. I'm still here.

Rituals don't have to be elaborate. They have to be consistent. A weekly walk. A shared playlist. A note in a lunch bag. A question you always ask before bed. These things create rhythm, safety, and a sense of "us" that life's chaos can't easily disrupt.

Renewal is the second part of the equation. The ability to choose each other again, especially when things feel stale or strained. That might mean a conversation about what's been missing. It might mean shaking up the routine. It might mean therapy, travel, or simply a night without distractions. But the act of choosing? Of saying, "Let's keep creating something together"? That's where long-term love breathes.

And perhaps most importantly, the small things require attention. Noticing. Slowing down enough to see the effort your partner made. To say thank you. To ask how they're doing and wait for the honest answer. It's not the big fights that wear most relationships down. It's the slow fade of appreciation. The assumption that love, once established, no longer needs tending.

But it does. Like a garden. Like anything living.

Because when the small things are tended, the big things take care of themselves. And long-term love, in the end, is not a destination. It's a daily practice. A ritual of choosing. A quiet, steady vow: "I still see you. And I still want to know you."

Case Study: Elise and Marcus – The Choosing Again

Elise and Marcus had been married for eighteen years. They'd raised two kids, started a business, grieved the loss of a parent, and weathered a few years where their marriage felt more like a shared task list than a romantic partnership. But through it all, they stayed, though not out of inertia, but out of choice.

Still, there was a period, around year fifteen, when things felt particularly fragile. They weren't fighting. They weren't connecting. Dinners were quiet. Conversations shallow. They stopped touching each other as they passed in the kitchen. When they sat on the couch, it was often with their phones in hand or a TV in the background.

Elise once told a friend, "It felt like living beside someone I used to be in love with."

One night, after putting the kids to bed and settling into their usual routine of parallel scrolling, Elise turned to Marcus and asked, "Do you still *see* me?"

He paused. Looked up. And instead of brushing it off or offering a quick reassurance, he said, "I think I've stopped looking."

That admission cracked something open, not in a painful way, but in a freeing one. They both cried. They talked for hours, not about dramatic problems but about the subtle erosion of attention. The way love, if not nurtured, slips into the background.

They didn't go to couples therapy. They didn't make a grand gesture. Instead, they made a new kind of promise: to choose each other again, not once, but daily.

They started having 15-minute check-ins at night. Sometimes it was about logistics, sometimes about feelings. They went for walks without their phones. They reinstituted Sunday coffee on the porch, something they hadn't done since before the kids came along. And perhaps most importantly, they began expressing gratitude again, not for grand acts, but for the tiny, invisible ones.

Three years later, their love doesn't look like it did when they first met. It looks steadier. More intentional. Less about excitement, more about presence.

Elise says, "People talk about long-term love like it's either passion or obligation. But really, it's practice. It's waking up each day and saying, 'Let's try again. I'm still here."

Reflection

Which daily ritual sustains your closest relationships, and which could you start?

Love doesn't always roar. Sometimes, it's the quiet persistence of staying.

Chapter 20: The Relationship With Yourself

The foundation beneath every connection you build, and the one you'll return to for the rest of your life.

Introduction

We spend so much of our lives trying to connect with partners, friends, family, and community. And yet, the most important relationship we'll ever have is the one we build with ourselves. It's the only one that never ends—the one we carry into every love, every argument, every silent night and hopeful morning.

This chapter is about that relationship. About how the way we treat ourselves shapes every other bond we form. About why self-awareness, self-compassion, and emotional maturity are not just personal goals, they're relational skills. Because the better we know and care for ourselves, the better we can love and be loved.

The Mirror You Can't Escape

Every relationship reflects you, but the one with yourself? It *is* you. It's the voice in your head when you mess up. The way you speak to your body. The stories you tell yourself about what you deserve. And yet, many of us don't realize we're in a relationship with ourselves until something breaks, until a partner leaves, a friendship ends, or the silence becomes too loud.

That's when we notice the shape of our inner world. Is it kind, or cruel? Is it grounded, or reactive? Do we know what we need, or just what we fear?

Your relationship with yourself sets the tone for everything else. If you don't believe you're worthy, you'll tolerate unkindness. If you don't know your values, you'll lose yourself in someone else's. If you can't sit with your feelings, you'll expect others to manage them for you or run from anyone who stirs them up.

But when you know yourself deeply, not just the curated version, but the whole truth, you stop needing relationships to rescue you. You stop looking for someone to fix you. You start choosing people from a place of clarity, not desperation.

This isn't about self-sufficiency to the point of isolation. It's about self and relationship as the starting point. The foundation. The place you return to when the world gets loud.

Solitude Isn't Emptiness

We often confuse solitude with loneliness. But they are not the same. Loneliness is the ache of disconnection. Solitude is the space where connection with the self begins.

When you're comfortable in your own company, everything shifts. You stop fearing the space between texts. You stop chasing validation. You stop needing every silence to be filled. You become more discerning, not because you're guarded, but because you know what peace feels like, and you're unwilling to trade it for chaos.

Spending time alone doesn't mean you don't want love. It means you're building a life where love is a complement, not a cure. Where a partner adds to your joy, not defines it, where affection feels like sunlight on your skin, not oxygen in your lungs.

Solitude allows you to hear your voice again. To notice what brings you alive. To meet your fears without fleeing. To rest in your presence without performing.

In this space, remember that you are not half looking for a whole. You are already whole. And the relationships that flourish from that place? They are not about completion. They are about connection. Expansion. Deep, mutual recognition.

Coming Home to Yourself

Perhaps the most crucial aspect of any relationship is the ability to return to your values when they're tested. Returning to your needs when they've been ignored. Returning to your center when you've drifted too far out, trying to be everything for everyone else.

Coming home to yourself isn't always peaceful. Sometimes it's messy. You might cry. You might rage. You might look in the mirror and not recognize who you've become. But slowly, with honesty and grace, you remember I am still here. I am still worthy. I am still becoming.

This home inside you, this relationship with yourself, is the place you can always begin again when love ends. When the world changes. When everything else is uncertain, this is where you learn to soothe yourself, to cheer for yourself, to ask, "What do I need now?" and wait for the answer.

And the more rooted you are here, the freer you become. Free to love without losing yourself. Free to be alone without fear. Free to build relationships that aren't about escaping but about expanding.

Because at the end of the day, every relationship you form will reflect, amplify, or challenge the one you have with yourself. And when that relationship is strong, honest, kind, and grounded, the rest will follow.

Case Study: River and the Mirror

River came out as non-binary in their late twenties, after years of trying to fit into gender roles that never felt right. They had been dating on and off since university, sometimes with men, sometimes with women, but something always felt... performative. Not because of the people they dated, but because they weren't fully present as themselves.

After coming out, River feared dating again. How do you explain your identity without becoming a lesson? How do you express needs when you're still learning them yourself?

Then came Jules.

They met at a queer bookshop. Jules asked thoughtful questions. Listened without fixing. On their second date, River said, "Sometimes I still feel like I need permission to take up space." Jules didn't try to reassure or romanticize. He said, "Thank you for telling me." And kept showing up.

The relationship wasn't perfect; River still had moments of dysphoria and still flinched when misgendered in public, but with Jules, they stopped apologizing for those moments. They began naming what they needed. And more importantly, they stopped performing the version of themselves they thought would be easier to love.

River says the turning point wasn't a big event. It was the first time they cried and didn't feel the urge to explain why. "I didn't need to be understood completely," they said. "I just needed to be accepted. And with him, I was."

Reflection

What's one thing you can do today to strengthen your relationship with yourself?

Self-love isn't a destination. It's a garden you tend with patience, even when no one's watching.

Chapter 21: The Rebuild

How to rebuild trust, worth, and clarity within yourself after heartbreak or years of self-abandonment.

Introduction

After love ends, or after years of bending yourself into shapes that don't fit, you may feel lost in questions of worth, direction, and purpose. Chapter 21 is your guide back to center. It's about repairing the relationship you have with yourself, so that no matter what happens next, you stand on solid ground. Here, you'll learn to mend wounds, reclaim your voice, and cultivate the resilience to choose connection, again and again, from a place of strength.

The Moment You Stop Pretending

The moment healing begins is rarely triumphant. More often, it's quiet. Awkward. It comes when you finally stop spinning the story in a way that lets you avoid the pain. It's when you say, not out loud but to yourself, *"Something inside me broke, and I haven't been okay since."*

For some, that fracture came in a flash, a betrayal, a betrayal you saw coming but hoped wouldn't arrive. For others, it came slowly, like a stone worn smooth by years of compromise and quiet self-erasure. You gave too much. You asked for too little. You played peacekeeper until the only person left unheard was you.

You don't always realize it at first. The absence creeps in around the edges. You don't laugh as much. Your voice grows uncertain. You start forgetting what you like, what you want, who you are. And then one day, perhaps in the middle of a perfectly ordinary afternoon, it catches up with you. You feel the ache of everything you've been carrying.

That's when something honest breaks through. I was hurt when... I lost myself by... I stopped believing I could...

It's not self-pity. It's recognition. You are not wallowing. You are witnessing. Naming the fracture isn't weakness; it's the first act of self-respect. It says, "I refuse to keep pretending this didn't matter." And in that refusal, the healing begins.

What You Gave Up Without Realizing

After the truth cracks open, another question often surfaces: *What else did I lose along the way?*

We talk about self-abandonment like it's a dramatic act. But most of the time, it's subtle. We stop asking for things. Stop dreaming. Stop defending the softest parts of ourselves. We turn down the volume on our needs, not because we don't have them, but because they didn't feel welcome in the rooms we occupied.

Maybe you gave up your mornings. Or your silence. Maybe you stopped writing, or laughing, or asking for affection in the way that makes you feel most known. You told yourself it was maturity. Or sacrifice. Or strength. But if you're honest, it was fear. Fear of being called too much. Too sensitive. Too selfish.

Now is the time to retrieve what was buried.

This is not about rage or regret, it's about excavation. Like a gentle archaeologist, you begin to unearth what's still alive inside you. The parts that never stopped wanting.

You sit quietly and ask: What do I crave? What do I need? What have I stopped allowing myself to want?
The answers might not come right away. But they're waiting. A boundary you once held. A joy you stopped claiming. A wish you buried but never stopped missing.

There will be answers. Maybe not right away. But they're there, waiting. A boundary you once held. A pleasure you stopped claiming. A wish you silenced.

This process isn't indulgent. It's foundational. You are laying the first bricks of a relationship with yourself that won't dissolve at the first sign of rejection. One that can stand.

The Practice of Returning

Awareness is a beginning, but it isn't the same as embodiment. You can know your wounds. You can name your longings. But unless those insights are woven into your days, they remain distant, intellectual, disembodied, abstract.

The fundamental shift happens through repetition. Through small acts that bring you back to yourself, over and over, until the returning becomes instinct.

Some of this might look quiet from the outside—a few words spoken into the mirror each morning, not for affirmation, but for recognition. You meet your own eyes and say something that lands: *"You belong here. You don't have to earn it."*

Or perhaps it takes shape in the way you begin to notice the moment your energy dips when someone asks something of you. This time, instead of swallowing your discomfort, you pause. You decline gently, firmly. You protect your peace, and then you acknowledge it, not with guilt, but with pride. *That was a new choice.*

In the evening, you might find a space in your day to reflect, not with pressure to document anything profound, but to quietly record one moment when you honored your own needs. A single line is enough. *I listened to myself. I didn't abandon what I knew.*

These small rituals are not about control. They are about re-establishing your presence in your own life. They don't need to be perfect, impressive, or even public. They need to be consistent enough to remind your nervous system that you are safe with yourself.

And over time, as they take root, something inside you steadies. You begin to trust your inner voice. Not because it's louder than everyone else's, but because you've stopped ignoring it.

That is how the rebuild becomes real. Not in dramatic leaps, but in these quiet moments of return. Again and again, until returning becomes your new way of staying.

Choosing Again

As your relationship with yourself regenerates, you'll reach new crossroads. Old patterns may beckon. Fear of loneliness may whisper. But now you have a choice informed by clarity, not desperation. Whether you step into a new connection, deepen self-exploration, or savor solitude, you do so from a place of agency.

You can ask: "Does this honor my needs?" "Does this align with my rebuilt values?" And if the answer is no, you have the strength to walk away with dignity, because you've already chosen yourself.

Rebuilding is not a one-time event, but an ongoing practice. Each day offers invitations to reaffirm your worth, renew your boundaries, and reclaim your voice. And in that practice, you discover that the most lasting love is the one you carry within.

Case Study: Joy and the Mirror

After her divorce, Joy felt broken. Her friends told her she was strong, but she didn't feel strong; she felt empty. She had spent 12 years making herself small inside someone else's expectations. Now, standing alone in her apartment, she didn't know who she was without them.

At first, she tried to rebuild by dating. By keeping busy. But every time she got close to someone new, she panicked. Not because they weren't kind, but because she hadn't yet returned to herself.

One morning, she wrote herself a letter. It began, *Dear Joy, I'm sorry I left you.* She cried for an hour. Then she made coffee. Then she read it aloud to the mirror.

That became her ritual. Each day, one small kindness: a meal cooked just for her. A boundary held. A walk taken without distraction. Slowly, her reflection changed, not physically, but energetically. She began to see someone worth returning to.

Joy says she's not "over it", but she is home again. And for the first time in years, she feels held. Not by another person. But by herself.

Reflection

What's your first ritual of reconnection going to be, and when will you begin it?

Becoming yourself is easier when someone's arms say, 'You're already enough."

Conclusion

Love Is the Work and the Reward

Love isn't a destination. It's not the finish line after you've done the "inner work," healed every wound, or found someone who finally "gets" you. Love is a practice, a daily returning, a choice, an ongoing act of presence.

By now, you've walked through the arc of connection: the way early experiences shape us, pulled toward certain people, challenged by difference, stretched by conflict, steadied by trust, and sometimes broken open by endings. You've seen how belonging, communication, sex, boundaries, and repair all interweave into something that looks like love, but only if we're willing to show up as we are, and let others do the same.

If there's one truth this book wants to leave you with, it's this: You are not behind. You are not broken. You are not unlovable because of the ways you've struggled or what you didn't learn until later. All of us are still learning. All of us are still building love, imperfectly, hopefully, with trembling hands and open hearts.

And here's the secret: love doesn't always feel like magic. Sometimes, it feels like showing up when it's easier to shut down. Sometimes, it's listening without fixing. Saying "I was wrong." Saying "I miss you." Saying "I need space." Sometimes, love is washing the dishes even when you're angry—or staying through the silence. Or leaving with kindness when staying would mean losing yourself.

Love isn't always a feeling. Sometimes, it's a decision. And in that decision is the deepest kind of freedom.

So take what speaks to you from these pages. Let go of what doesn't. And most importantly, keep practicing. Whether you're loving a partner, a friend, a parent, a child, or learning how to love yourself all over again, know this: the work is worth it. And so are you.

About the Author

C.S. Morgan writes about the heart—with clarity, compassion, and the kind of hard-won wisdom that comes from loving deeply and losing honestly. A lifelong observer of human connection, Morgan blends narrative insight with emotional precision to explore how we relate, repair, and return to ourselves.

Their work invites readers to slow down, reflect, and reconnect with the truths that live beneath the surface. Whether writing about long-term love, identity, or the quiet courage of beginning again, Morgan's voice feels like a conversation with someone who sees you clearly—and stays.

When not writing, they can often be found with a dog-eared novel, a strong cup of coffee, and an open seat beside them— offering space for whatever story comes.

About the Publisher

Welcome to The Book On Publishing

At The Book On Publishing, we believe in rewriting the rules of learning. Whether you're chasing your next big idea, building a better life, or simply curious about what should have been taught in school, you've come to the right place.

We're a platform built for dreamers, doers, and lifelong learners—offering bold, practical books and tools that empower you to take charge of your journey. From real-world skills to mindset mastery, we publish the book on what matters.

No fluff. No lectures. Just what you need to know, delivered with clarity, purpose, and a spark of curiosity.

Start exploring. Start growing. Start writing your story.

Read more at https://thebookon.ca.

Acknowledgment of AI Assistance

Portions of this book were developed with the support of ChatGPT, an AI language model created by OpenAI. While every word has been carefully reviewed and refined by the author, ChatGPT served as a valuable tool for brainstorming, editing, and structuring ideas. Its assistance helped accelerate the creative process and bring clarity to complex topics.